Fundamentals of
Sociology
of
Education
With Reference to Africa

Fundamentals of
Sociology
of
Education

With Reference to Africa

Lucy Wairimu Kibera
Agnes Kimokoti

University of Nairobi Press

First Published 2007 by
University of Nairobi Press
Jomo Kenyatta Memorial Library, University of Nairobi
P.O. Box 30197
Nairobi, Kenya
E-mail: nup@uonbi.ac.ke
Website: www.uonbi.ac.ke/press

The University of Nairobi Press supports and furthers University of Nairobi's objectives of discovery, dissemination and preservation of knowledge, and of stimulating intellectual and cultural life by publishing works of the highest quality in association with partners in different parts of the world. In doing so, it adheres to the University's tradition of excellence, innovation, and scholarship.

© University of Nairobi Press, 2007
The moral rights of the authors have been asserted.

All rights reserved. Except for the quotation of fully acknowledged short passages for the purposes of critique review, research or teaching, no part of this publication may be reproduced, stored in any retrieval system, or transmitted in any form or means without a prior written permission from the University of Nairobi Press.

University of Nairobi Library CIP Data

Kibera, Lucy Wairimu
    Fundamentals of Sociology of Education
    With Reference to Africa
    by L.W. Kibera and A. Kimokoti
    Nairobi: University of Nairobi Press, 2007.
LC 191.8 .A35K5
1. Educational Sociology –Africa.
I. Title . II. Kimokoti, Agnes

ISBN 9966 846 81 6

Printed by
Starbright Services Ltd
Nairobi

Table of Content

Preface xi

1. Sociology 1

Definition of Sociology 1
Development of Sociology.. 3
Scope of Sociology 13
Sociological Theory 13
Sociology and Other Social Sciences 14
Sociology and Anthropology 15
Psychology and Sociology 15
Economics and Sociology 15
Political Science and Sociology 16
Summary 16
Study Questions 16
References 16

2. Origins and Development of Sociology of Education 19

What is Sociology of Education? 19
Origins and Development of Sociology of Education 19
Educational Sociology and Sociology of Education 25
Concerns of Sociology of Education 26
Summary 27
Study Questions 27
References 28

3. Sociological Theories and their Application to Education 29

Definition of Sociological Theories... 29
Sociological Theories of Education 29
Structural-Functionalism/Consensus 29
Conflict Theory 35
Symbolic Interaction Theory 39
Ethnomethodology Theory 43
Feminist theories and education 44

Liberal Feminism 45
Marxist Socialist Feminism 46
Radical Feminism 47
Summary 50
Study Questions 52
References 52

4. Socialization and Education 55

Meaning of Socialization 55
Process of Socialisation 55
Agents of Socialization 59
Socialization and Education 65
Summary 66
Study questions 66
References 67

5. Role and Purpose of Indigenous Education 69

The Concept of African Indigenous Education 69
Goals of African Indigenous Education 70
The Curriculum 71
Methods of Instruction 72
Decline of Indigenous Education 73
Indigenous Education Versus Western Education 74
Summary 75
Study Questions 75
References 76

6. Moral Education Among African Indigenous Societies in Pre-colonial Era 77

Concepts of Morality and Moral Education 77
Definition of Moral Education 77
Aims of Moral Education among African Indigenous
Societies 79
Agents of Moral Education among the African
Indigenous Peoples 81
Reasons for the Success of Moral Education in
Pre-colonial Africa 83

Challenges of Teaching Moral Education in Modern
Africa 84
Summary 86
Study questions 88
References..88

7. Culture and Education 91

The Concept of Culture...91
Causes of Cultural Change 93
Content of Culture 96
Characteristics of culture 98
Education and Cultural Transmission...................................99
Culture and the School Curriculum 102
Summary 104
Study questions 105
References..105

8. Education and Social Stratification 107

Definition of Social Stratification.......................................107
Definitions of Social Class 111
Social Class and Equality of Educational Opportunity 112
The Influence of Social Class on School Academic
Performance 113
Summary 119
Study questions 120
References..120

9. The Sociology of the Classroom 123

The Characteristics of the Classroom 123
Patterns of Teacher-Pupil Interactions................................123
Teaching Methods and their Influence on
Teacher-Pupil Interactions in the Classroom......................127
Teacher Expectations and Students' Academic
Performance 129
Teacher and Classroom Management.................................131
Authority and Discipline..131
Interaction Dynamics in the Classroom.............................133

Summary 137
Study Questions 138
References... 138

10. Gender and Education 141

Concept of Gender and Sex 141
The Ideology of Sexism...143
Gender Disparity in Education 143
Factors that Affect the Education of Girls.............................147
Gender and the Hidden Curriculum.......................................150
Gender, Education and Employment Opportunities..............153
Outcomes of Under-Representation of Female Student
at all Levels of Kenya's Educational System 153
Some Ways of Improving the Educational,
Occupational, and Leadership Chances of Women...............154
Summary 156
Study Questions 156
References...156

11. The Teacher and the Teaching Profession 159

Is Teaching a Profession? 159
Characteristics of a Profession...160
Why do People Choose Teaching as a Career? 163
Categories of Teachers in Kenya's School System 164
Why most People do not Choose Teaching as a Career 165
The Changing Multiple Roles of the Teacher........................166
The Roles of the Teacher within the School..........................166
Teacher's Role within the Community...................................169
Conflict in Social Roles of the Teacher.................................169
Perception of the Teacher by the Students 170
Summary 171
Study Questions 172
References...172

12. Who Joins the Teaching Profession? *A Case Study of Undergraduate Students' Attitudes and Perceptions Towards the Teaching Profession*..**173**

Introduction...173
What is Teacher Education?..174
Characteristics of Individuals who Join the Teaching Profession..175
Presentation of Findings 177
Student teachers' attitudes and perceptions of the teaching profession 180
The Status of the Teaching Profession in Kenya.....................185
Ways of Improving the Teaching Profession..........................188
Study questions 189
References...189

Glossary **191**

Appendix..**196**

Index **199**

Preface

Children grow up in several and different environments; home, school, community and religious organizations provide experiences from which children acquire and develop skills, attitudes and attachments which characterize them as individuals and shape their choice and performance of adult roles.

This book is about practices and processes involved in socialization and education, particularly the agencies concerned with the ways in which schools, through their teachers, curricula and organization, deliberately and/or informally influence the young.

Among all agencies of socialization, schools are in a strong position to exert influence upon the young. This stems in part from their specialized functions and expertise concerning scholastic and technical instruction. Schools introduce forms of authority to students, social and working relationships and occupational roles. Some of this influence is specific and overt, operating through deliberate instruction to more or less determined objectives.

Although there is much emphasis on schools and their students, it would make little sense to discuss schools in isolation from other agencies of socialization. Consequently, we have discussed the influence of other socialising agencies such as home, peers, media and religious organizations, school processes, and practices on educational outcomes. By doing this, it is hoped that the influence of each socialization agent has been put in its proper perspective and that its limitations can be appreciated.

The first chapter discusses the development of sociology as a discipline and some of its various branches. Chapter 2 deals specifically with the origins and development of sociology of education and its concerns. Sociological theories and their application to education are contained in Chapter 3. Chapter 4 looks at socialization, particularly, the agents of socialization and the relationships between socialization and education. Chapter 5 discusses the role and purpose of indigenous education while Chapter

6 examines how moral education was imparted on the young during pre-colonial era. Chapter 7 examines the relationship between culture and education.

Culture is the main content of curriculum of any education system while education is seen as a major agent of development. However, as much as education is viewed as an instrument of social and economic development, it contributes in some ways to social inequality. Chapter 8 therefore discusses education and social stratification. Chapter 9 looks at the sociology of the classroom by examining its complex environment. Chapter 10 highlights the factors affecting the education of girls while chapter 11 discusses the teacher and teaching profession and the changing multiple roles of the teacher in response to societal changes. Finally, Chapter 12 is a case study of the attitudes of Kenyan undergraduate students and perceptions towards the teaching profession.

It is our hope that students of sociology of education will find this book resourceful in the course of their study.

Lucy Wairimu Kibera
Agnes Kimokoti
May 2007

1

Sociology

Introduction

Although this is an introductory text to sociology of education, that is, the study of relationship between the institution of education and the society, it is imperative we briefly discuss sociology as a discipline. The reason for discussing it as a discipline is that sociology of education applies sociological methods of investigation such as measurement, observation, experimentation and sociological theoretical frameworks like functionalist, conflict and symbolic interactionist perspectives, among others, in examining variables that affect education and its structure.

Definition of Sociology

Sociology has been defined in several ways. Auguste Comte (1798-1857), founder of the discipline of sociology, said that sociology is the study of interaction between human institutions, such as the family, education, religion as well as their development and the manner of transformation of societies. Comte emphasized that society must be seen as a whole. On the other hand, Max Weber defined sociology as "a science which attempts the interpretative understanding of social action in order to arrive at a causal explanation of its course and effects." According to Max Weber, the term social action referred to any human behaviour to which acting individuals attain subjective meaning.

On the basis of these definitions, it can be concluded that sociology is the study of human behaviour in groups. Ballantine (1989), suggested that sociology could be divided into studies of institutions in the society, studies of processes and studies of other group related situations. The structure of society is represented by family, religion, education, politics and economics. Formal organizations such as schools are part of the institutional society while processes are the action part of the society. Some of the examples of processes include socialisation and education.

Given that sociology is the study of social institutions and human behaviour in groups, it is apparent that its study would be impossible without society. The term society refers to a congregation of human beings who share a common cultural heritage in terms of language and inhabitancy of a specific geographical region. For instance, tribes living in Kenya as citizens share, to a large extent, common political ideology and way of life. The survival of a society depends on its ability to produce children and to induct them into the ways of the society. The continuity of a society is assured when every member of that society participates in the activities of the society in accordance with that society's expectations. Thus, members of the society must fit and operate within social groups or social systems such as the family, religious institutions, school, government and economic structures.

Every individual in the society has specific roles to play within those social systems. For instance, a secondary school, which forms part of the educational social system and also an interdependent part of the larger society, must educate children under its care along prescribed values of the society. In realization of the goals of the secondary school teachers, pupils and the support staff are expected to work together towards the achievement of the stipulated goals. The government, on the other hand, provides an enabling economic environment. In addition, it protects members of the society from both internal and external enemies.

Development of Sociology

Sociology is the youngest of the social sciences and like all the other fields of knowledge, it is an offspring of philosophy. Simply defined, philosophy is the study of knowledge. Sociology became recognized as a discipline in the nineteenth century. It developed as a response to problems in Western Europe brought about by two types of revolutions. These revolutions were the French revolution and the Industrial revolution. In France, between 1789 and 1812, peasants revolted against the aristocrats because they denied them political, material and social rights as citizens. The aristocrats controlled the government and resources including land. The peasants were only allowed to use land by the ruling class in return for services to them such as military and domestic services.

The French revolution, often referred to as a democratic revolution, led to the murder of the French King, disorganization of society and introduction of democratic practices. During this time, industrial revolution was taking place in Britain. Technological advances led to reduced labour workforce. As a result, unemployment, social upheaval, and crimes increased. Industrialization also brought about urbanization, overcrowding in cities and towns, separation of family members, that is, those working in cities, towns and job seekers from their rural based folks.

Movement of peoples affected family unity. The scholars of the time, such as Auguste Comte, Herbert Spencer, Emile Durkheim and Max Weber, believed that the discipline of sociology would help people to re-establish order in the society. A brief account of their views on society and the role of the discipline of sociology in social reconstruction are outlined next.

Auguste Comte (1798-1857) a French Philosopher, is said to have coined the term sociology from the Latin word *socio* meaning society, and a Greek word *logy*, which stands for science, in 1838. Thus sociology came to be associated with the study of society.

Comte lived during and after the French revolution. The French revolution brought with it disorder, material and cultural poverty. Industrial revolution, which was taking place in Europe at the time also, contributed to the breakdown of agricultural way of life that was simple and integrative. Industrial revolution sparked off movements of people from rural areas to industrial centres which resulted in breakdown of family ties, moral degradation and defiance of customs that had bound people together for many centuries. Comte was distressed by the negative social changes that accompanied the two revolutions. He wanted to replace disorder with social order through total reconstruction of society. He contended that social events were not the result of accident and that they could be rationally ordered and controlled through concerted effort. He suggested that the discipline of sociology would provide people with the necessary knowledge for reconstruction and establishment of order in the society. In 1842, Comte launched his book entitled Positive Philosophy. He believed that positivism or study of society using scientific methods, would help to bring out "social facts" that would facilitate reconstruction of society.

According to Comte, positivism is a system of philosophy which examines the phenomena around us through the senses. It states that all knowledge must be supported by facts. Therefore, facts that are not verifiable by observation through the senses do not constitute knowledge. Positivism further employs human reason in the organization and interpretation of the observed phenomena. It also holds that what has been observed accurately by one scientist should be able to be replicated by others studying the same issue.

Comte identified two broad fields of study in sociology; social statics and social dynamics. These two concepts represent a basic division in the discipline of sociology which appears in many different forms throughout the history of sociology up to today. Social statics is the study of various institutions of the society, for instance, the economy, government, family, churches and other institutions and their interrelatedness to each other. Comte looks at the statical study of sociology which deals with the investigation of laws of action and reaction of the different parts of the social system. Social dynamics, on the other hand, is the study of how societies developed and changed over time. Comte believed that all societies moved through certain fixed stages of development, from primitive age towards an increasing perfection. These stages are theological, metaphysical and positive stages and each of the stages marked a phase of intellectual development.

(a) Theological Stage

The priestly class dominated this stage of development. The dominant culture was military conquest, slavery, beliefs in many gods, devils and angels and supernaturalism.

(b) Metaphysical Stage

This stage was characterized by use of rationality in analyzing social happenings. People pursued meanings and explanations of terms. The society was more orderly and rule of law prevailed and provided a secure basis for co-operative civil life.

(c) Positive Stage

In this stage, people rejected explanations based on supernaturalism and metaphysical explanations that could not be supported by facts. Comte believed that all knowledge was human knowledge and that it was based on human thought. In a scientific age, society could only be held by laws based on facts. There was emphasis on the use of empirical methods in studying society such as experimentation and observation. Comte believed that human reason was capable of creating and restoring social order. The problems accompanying industrialization had been people-created and could therefore be solved or overcome through application of human mind. Comte further contended that the discipline of sociology, through employing proven scientific methods such as experimentation, observation, measurements and generalization in the study of society, would help in the understanding and explanation of social events or happenings.

Auguste Comte's Contribution to Sociology

(i) He founded the discipline of sociology.
(ii) He recommended the use and application of scientific methods in the study of society.
(iii) He identified two broad fields of sociology namely: social statics and social dynamics.

Shortcomings of Comte's Conception of Society

Comte contended that all societies progressed through fixed stages. However, it is noted that all societies do not need to evolve through all the stages of development because cultures borrow some material as well as ideological aspects through diffusion. He also looked at society from a unilinear perspective.

Herbert Spencer (1820-1903) was a British scholar who believed that society progressed through various socio-cultural stages, that is, from primitive tribal societies which were, on the whole, homogenous, to large-scale industrial heterogeneous societies. Spencer, a social evolutionist, likened society to an organism whose parts – institutions – function together harmoniously to form an integrated whole. Society is a resemblance of human body organs, which work to sustain it, for example the heart, brain, lungs, kidneys and others must function in harmony for the body to be in good health. Similarly, different institutions of the society must work together to sustain it. Thinkers like Spencer were labelled as functionalist. His evolutionary theory of societies was influenced by ideas of Charles Darwin, a believer in evolution of species. According to Darwin, weak species die while strong ones survive.

Spencer likened the survival of strong species to the survival of strong societies. To Spencer, weak societies and individuals will perish while strong ones will survive. He concluded that the wealth of the "haves" was an evidence of their natural superiority over the "have-nots" (propertyless). Therefore, re-distribution of wealth and power by providing services such as public welfare and public education was seen by him as interference of social evolution for it promoted the interests of the weak at the expense of the strong. Spencer's conception of society would condemn giving help to disadvantaged groups in the society for this would translate to what he termed as "social engineering".

Contributions of Spencer to Sociology

He identified the following areas of study family, politics, religion, social control, restraints, rules and regulations, industry and work. Spencer stressed the need for sociological study of associations, communities, division of labour, social differentiation, social stratification, sociology of knowledge, sciences and the study of art and aesthetics. He emphasized that Sociology was the study of the interrelatedness between various units of the society – issues like how education is related to family life, morality, economy and all other social institutions.

Criticism of Spencer's understanding of society

His theory was against the weak and disadvantaged in the society. His ideas about society had been greatly influenced by Darwin's theory of evolution which showed that some species had become extinct on account of their failure to adapt to the environment. Similarly, he contended that weak societies would perish while strong ones would survive.

Emile Durkheim (1858-1917) was a French scholar who defined sociology as the science of society. He maintained that society is a reality and that it exists independent of the individual. The existence of the society is reflected in its beliefs, codes of human conduct and ideals. He stated that man is who he is (human being) because he/she lives in a society.

Durkheim emphasized the importance of analyzing the relationships among institutions and between them and their social-cultural settings. He referred to various aspects of the society and human conduct as social facts. Social facts act outside us to bring human beings in line with the moral demands of the society. Durkheim resisted the psychological approach that places individual action above society. To him, it is the society, which makes individuals behave the way they do and society is held together by traditions, common beliefs and values. He termed these as the collective conscience, the social glue that bound people together. Society itself is made up of the synthesis of the consciences, thoughts, and wills of individuals. This conscience is not simply the conscience of the individual thoughts. It is an integrated synthesis of these thoughts that he called collective conscience. To him, society is autonomous. It exists independently of the will of any other individual. Using this line of thought, Durkheim attributed human acts not to individuals' decisions and wills but to society. For example, he viewed the phenomenon of suicide not as an individual act but as a social fact forced on the individual by societal forces. Using this theory, he was able to study the occurrences of suicide among people of different races, and religions. From his analysis of records in France and elsewhere in Europe, Durkheim noticed that people in certain social categories had lower rates of suicide than others. For example, he established that:

- Fewer Jews committed suicide than Catholics;
- Fewer Catholics than Protestants committed suicide;
- Fewer married people than single ones committed suicide.
- Fewer civilians than those in military service committed suicide.

From these findings, he concluded that rates of suicide seemed directly related to differing levels of social cohesion. Durkheim hypothesized that the higher the degree of social cohesion, the less likely individuals would take their own lives except in the case of over-integration. He identified three types of suicide. These included altruistic suicide, egoistic suicide, and anomic suicide.

(i) *Altruistic suicide*: This suicide results from over-integration of an individual into the group life. That is, the norms and moral codes of the group are what absolutely guide one's life or processes of action. Thus, to die for the group is to find fulfillment in the group. This may explain suicidal missions whereby individuals give up their lives for group goals; for instance, peoples' right to self-determination. This kind of behaviour is common among Arabs in the Middle East, especially the Palestines.

(ii) *Egoistic suicide*: A person who is not strongly involved with his group and who is rather alienated from it becomes self-centred and does not have emotional support that makes life a joy. People who are egocentric are likely to commit suicide because they feel lonely.

(iii) *Anomic suicide*: Occurs where roles or guides to behaviour of members do not exist. Members become disoriented. Such people find no meaning in life. For instance, rapid industrialization in many parts of Africa has resulted in rapid changes in the structure of the society. In the process, traditional authority, customs, and morality have been undermined.

Durkheim also identified two types of societies. These included mechanical and organic solidarity societies. He conceptualized mechanical societies as primitive and folk type of societies. People in these societies relate to each other almost in everything. This kind of relationship exists today in a family to a great extent, and it is characterized by deep feelings and a desire to share everything. Mechanical societies are integrative. Modern societies or organic solidarity or industrial societies are held together by a web or network of relationships based on contracts. In modern societies, contracts are governed by the law. Durkheim on the whole describes modern societies as disintegrative.

Contributions of Durkheim to Sociology

- He was one of the earliest scholars to use empirical method to study the society.
- He developed the sociological theory of social cohesion and he demonstrated the impact of social cohesion on society through his study of suicide as a social phenomenon.
- He developed the sociological concepts of social facts. These stand for different aspects of social phenomena; for instance, laws, family, and education and so on.
- He identified areas of study in sociology as:
  (i) General sociology, which included personality of the individual as well as collective personality.
  (ii) Sociology of religion.
  (iii) Sociology of law and morals, political organizations, social organizations, marriage and family.
  (iv) Sociology of the crime.
  (v) Sociology of economics including subsections on the measurement of value and on occupational groups.
  (vi) Demography or study of population figures.
  (vii) Sociology of aesthetics or values and morality.

Max Weber (1864-1920) was a German sociologist and economist. According to Weber, sociology is "a science which attempts the interpretative understanding of *social action* in order to arrive at a causal explanation of its course and effects". Max Weber regarded the term "social action" as all human behaviour to which acting individuals attach subjective meaning.

Max Weber wrote extensively on religion, economic life, including money, division of labour, bureaucracy and large-scale organizations. In his work on religion, he tried to examine the effect of religious ideas on economic activities and social stratification. He published an essay entitled *The Protestant Ethic and Spirit of Capitalism* (1904 - 1905). He explained various Christian beliefs and material possessions. Protestant religion, according to Weber, emphasized that there was no conflict between material possession and salvation. The possession of lots of material resources was viewed as a manifestation that God rewarded hard work. In contrast, Catholicism stressed repentance of sin and it did not place a high value on ambition, wealth, and success on earth. Indeed, Protestants in Kenya embrace mechanical methods of contraception while majority of Catholics do not and therefore have more children.

Weber also came up with the concept of bureaucratisation. This concept is concerned with the organization and co-ordination of human activities rationally on basis of rules, qualifications, experiences, and positions of authority rather than persons of authority, in order to achieve the greatest amount of productivity in modern economies. He believed that society would be run through rational principles that allowed little or no room for emotional concerns or individual differences. He is also credited with identifying three distinct types of leadership, namely: *charismatic, traditional* and *bureaucratic legal* authority. These types of authority provide the relationships between a supreme ruler, for instance, a prophet, a king, or a parliament.

Under charismatic domination, the ruler's exercise of authority rests on extraordinary and magnetic qualities, which both he and his followers believe to be inspired by some transcendent/super-natural power. Examples of charismatic leaders include, Mahatma Gandhi,

Jomo Kenyatta, prophet Mohamed, and Jesus Christ. On the other hand, in traditional domination, the rulers are bound by immemorial custom that also sanctions their right to the arbitrary exercise of their will. Under legal domination, the exercise of authority is subject to a system of generalized rules.

Weber held that if rulers fail to justify their domination in terms of charisma, tradition or law, they tend to undermine the belief in these standards among officials and the public at large, and when this happens, such domination is likely to change. Thus, under charismatic domination, belief in the very existence of charisma may be undermined by rulers' excessive claims to miraculous attributes or by too insistent demands by his followers that he gives proof of such attributes. Similarly, too much arbitrariness can undermine the authority of the sacred tradition that justifies the domination of the traditional ruler. And for the rule of law to endure, it is essential that rules appear to apply to all, rulers and the ruled.

Karl Marx (1818 - 1883) was a German scholar. Although he was not considered to be a sociologist, his ideas have had a profound effect on the field of sociology. Karl Marx's ideas predicted an impeding revolution due to class conflict between the rich capitalists and the poor working class. This made him "persona non grata" in his country. He sought refuge in Paris, France from 1843, then to Brussels, Belgium 1845-1849, and finally to London, Britain where he lived until his death in 1883.

He believed that human history and society are products of economic forces. He asserted that the history of human society is the history of the struggle between people of different social classes. Karl Marx, in his *Communist Manifesto* published in 1848, stated that societies were divided into two classes, that is, the "haves" or the bourgeoisie, and the "have nots" or proletariat. The bourgeoisie are owners of means of production, factories, machines and capital. The workers, proletariats, or the have nots, own nothing but labour "(living labour)" which they sell at prices set by capitalists. These classes emerged clearly after the industrial revolution. He felt that the worker was alienated from the means of production in which "dead capital" or "dead labour" dominated the "living labour", the worker. He expressed these ideas in his book called *Capital*.

Karl Marx contended that society was infested with conflicts rather than integrative tendencies. Conflicts in Marx's opinion were those of economic nature. Conflicts force the society to move from one stage to another. For instance, the French Revolution forced society from feudalism and autocracy to democratic institutions where people had a say in the government through elected representatives. Likewise, Karl Marx argued that capitalism would give birth to socialism. He believed that capitalists would continue to exploit workers or proletariats, in their quest to amass wealth. In the process, the gap between the haves and have nots would become too wide for workers to bear. Consequently, workers of the world would unite and overthrow capitalists and their governments. He claimed that such governments only protected the interests of capitalists. The workers would take over ownership of equipment, factories and would thereafter share out the products of their labour equally. With socialism, governments would be rendered irrelevant. To Karl Marx, governments only existed to protect capitalists and the governing class. Thus, in the event of socialism replacing capitalism, government would be replaced by series of associations to manage the production, distribution of goods and provision of services. Socialism as a system aims at providing the "greatest happiness to the greatest number".

Between mid nineteenth century and early twentieth century, socialism was a very powerful movement especially in the Soviet Union, Eastern Europe and China. African countries too embraced socialism to varying degrees in the late 1950`s and early 1960`s when they gained independence. However, with the fall of the Soviet Union, socialism declined tremendously in 1990s.

The major shortcoming of socialism was that workers of the world did not unite to overthrow capitalism as predicted by Karl Marx. This is attributed to the fact that capitalists gradually improved the working conditions of workers and their remunerations. Again, where socialism emerged, for instance, in the Soviet Union and Eastern Europe communist states, it did not seem to generate enough wealth for distribution to all its citizens. This was attributed to the fact that workers did not feel motivated enough to work for the good of others. In turn, socialist governments also become oppressive in their attempt to force workers to become productive.

The maturation of the working class was not able to keep up with the rapid expansion of capitalist system, as Max had hoped. Maximilian (1975) suggested that societies should embrace a rationalised economic social order on a worldwide scale, otherwise, they will be faced with gradual self-destruction that may lead to a state of "barbaric chaos". The poor, for example, will unlikely succumb to poverty–induced death without a fight. In time, they may make the lives of the "haves" or the wealthy, unbearable. The rate of violent crimes which is often associated with poverty is steadily rising in less industrialised economies like Kenya. Falling enrolment rates of children in school is another evidence of poverty. It is hoped that introduction of free primary education in Kenya in January, 2003 will improve school enrolment rates. Needless to say, that intention may still pose a problem because school uniform, transport to and from school, and lunch while at school are not free.

Scope of Sociology

The broad areas of study in Sociology are: Sociological Theory; Sociology of History; Sociology of the Family; Sociology of Religion and Sociology of Education. These areas of study with regard to sociology are by no means exhaustive. Other branches of Sociology are: Industrial Sociology, Human Ecology and Demography, Sociology of Music, Sociology of Language, Sociology of Art and Literature, Political Sociology and Mathematical Sociology, Political Sociology, Military Sociology, Rural Sociology. Though sociology has many areas of study, only sociological theory shall be briefly discussed here because it has a lot of relevance to Sociology of Education as we shall see later.

Sociological Theory

A *theory* refers to a statement of general principles, which try to explain the nature of things. A sociological theory is therefore, a branch of sociology that attempts to explain patterns of behaviour in the society. It tries to answer questions such as, why people in society behave the way they do. How and why social classes came to be formed in societies, and how social change occurs. Sociological theories, therefore, endeavour to organize facts, ideas, concepts and principles in order to explain patterns of behaviour in a society. There are several sociological theories, which attempt to explain the nature of society. These theories include: functional or consensus theory; conflict theory; symbolic interaction theory; exchange theory; and ethno methodology theory. These sociological theories are discussed in Chapter 3.

Sociology and Other Social Sciences

As mentioned earlier, sociology is one of the disciplines of the social sciences. Social sciences refer to various disciplines that focus their attention on specific aspects of society. These disciplines include: anthropology, demography, economics, political science, psychology, history and human geography. In our discussion, we shall only examine the relationship between a few of them that is, anthropology, psychology, economics and political science.

The term *science* stands for knowledge of facts about a phenomenon, which have been gained and verified by exact observation, organized experiment and ordered thinking. Scientific knowledge, therefore, is acquired through scientific methods. A scientific method is an approach or a strategy of investigation; a method grounded in the notion of empiricism. *Empiricism* is defined as pursuit of knowledge through observation and experiment. Thus beliefs, superstitions and misinformation are not part of science because they are not verifiable. The facts of science are based upon specific empirical observations or proofs. All science rest on certain assumptions, that:

- Reality, that is, the world, both physical and social, exists.
- Knowledge of reality is obtainable via human senses.
- The world is orderly and there are causes and effects to explain the physical as well as the social phenomena.

- The most valid method of checking knowledge is through the independent conclusions of a number of competent observers. Consequently, scientists cannot accept what other competent observers cannot validate as part of scientific knowledge.

Sociology and Anthropology

Anthropology is partly a biological and partly a social science discipline. Physical anthropology deals with the origins of man and variations in human species, including the study of race. Social and cultural anthropology on the other hand, concentrate on the study of culture and ways of life among the preliterate communities throughout the world.

Psychology and Sociology

Psychology is defined as the science of the mind or of mental processes encompassing the study of the capacities of the mind that receive sensations, give them meaning, and respond to them. However, psychologists have recognized the need to investigate interpersonal relations and group membership. This has led to emergence of social psychology.

Social psychology is largely concerned with connections between group experience and the individual behaviour and personality. Social psychology involves any study of social processes which systematically considers how the psychological properties of every individual human being or personality dispositions of particular individuals, acting in a particular situation, influence the outcome of social process.

Economics and Sociology

Economics is the study of the production and distribution of goods and services. It deals with phenomena of cost and price, of savings and investment, of supply and demand. The economist further explores how economic order is related to and dependent upon many non—economic forces, including government, public opinion, family life and migration. Sociologists help us to study these relations and also try to establish their importance for industrial stability and social change.

Political Science and Sociology

Political science or government consists mainly of two elements; political theory and administration. Political theory usually examines ideas about government from the earliest times to the present, while the administration describes the formal structure and functions of government agencies.

However, neither political theory nor government administration gives extended attention to political behaviour. Political sociology, on the other hand, investigates various aspects of political behaviour such as voting, popular attitudes and values about political issues, the membership of political movements, voluntary organizations, and the process of decision making within small and inside large private and government institutions.

Summary

The chapter has defined sociology as the scientific study of human behaviour in groups. It has also traced the origin and development of sociology in the nineteenth century and saw it as an offshoot of the French political revolution and industrial revolution of Britain, which brought dis-equilibrium in the social order. The sociology discipline was expected to come up with strategies of re-establishing social order within the changed social structures. Finally, the relationship between sociology and other social sciences has been highlighted.

Study Questions

1. Define the concept of "sociology". Explain why sociology as a discipline became prominent in the nineteenth century.

2. Discuss the contributions of Auguste Comte, Herbert Spencer, and Emile Durkheim in the founding of the discipline of sociology.

References

Ballantine, Jeanne H. (1989). *The Sociology of Education.* New Jersey: Prentice Hall Inc. Second Edition.

Ezewu, Edward. (1983). *Sociology of Education.* London: Longman.

Inkeles, Alex. (1987). *What is Sociology? An Introduction to the Discipline and Profession.* New Delhi: Prentice Hall of India Private Limited.

Kamotho, J. (1996). School Entrants drop: Enrolment downby 13 percent", in *Daily Nation.* Nairobi: Tuesday 16th July.

Marx, Karl. (1884). *The Community Manifesto.* London: Penguin Books.

Maximillian, Rubel and Manale, Margaret. (1975). *Marx without Myth London:* Basil Blackwell.

Morrish, Ivor. (1978). *The Sociology of Education. An Introduction. London: George Allen and Unwin. Second Edition.*

Republic of Kenya. (1997 - 2001). *National Development Plan.* Nairobi: Government Printer.

2

Origins and Development of Sociology of Education

What is Sociology of Education?

Sociology of Education is a branch of sociology, which studies how social institutions affect educational processes and outcomes. It investigates the functions of education, that is, what education does, its methods, institutions, administration and curricula in relation to other parts of the society such as the economy, government, religion and the family. Sociology of Education also seeks to establish the influence of socio-cultural forces such as religion, beliefs, traditions and cultural heritage in general on the educational outcomes and development of personality. The understanding of the goals and means of educational socialization processes differs according to the sociological and theoretical orientation or paradigm used. These theories and their corresponding interpretation of educational processes such as conflict, symbolic interaction and structural functions are discussed in chapter three.

Origins and Development of Sociology of Education

The origin and development of Sociology of Education is associated with a number of scholars such as Emile Durkheim, Karl Mannheim and John Dewey. *Emile Durkheim (1858 - 1917)* was a distinguished French scholar. He attended the famous Ecole Normale Superieure institution in Paris. On completion, he taught in several schools.

Fundamentals of Sociology of Education

From 1885 – 1886, he took study leave and went to study in Germany. On his return home, he was awarded a professorship in Sociology and Education in 1887 at Bordeaux, where he remained until 1902. While at Bordeaux he wrote three books: *Division of Labour* (1893), *The Rules of Sociological Method* (1895), and *Suicide* (1897). He also founded and edited the journal, *L,anne'e Sociologique*. In 1902, he was awarded professorship in Sociology and Education at Sorbonne in Paris and in the same year, he became the chair for education at Sorbonne. Durkheim was among the first scholars to introduce sociology of education into the training of teachers. He defined education as an influence exercised by adult generations on those not yet ready for social life. Education, therefore, is expected to arouse and develop in the children certain number of physical, intellectual and moral states which are demanded of them by both the political society as a whole and the special milieu for which they are specifically destined.

Durkheim further argued that education was specific to a particular society and its major purpose was to create some homogeneity and therefore, co-operation among its members. This in turn guaranteed the survival of the society:

> It is society as a whole and each particular millieu that determine that ideal that education realises. Society can survive only if there exists among its members a sufficient degree of homogeneity; education perpetuates and reinforces this homogeneity by fixing in the child, from the beginning, the essential similarities that collective life demands. But on the other hand, without certain diversity, all co-operation would be impossible; education ensures the persistence of this necessary diversity by being itself diversified and specialized. (Durkheim, 1956).

From this quotation, it is apparent Durkheim expected education:

- To transform the individual from the state of being asocial into a social being. A social person is one who has not yet been socialised or does not yet know or internalised their society's ways of life, while a social being has been initiated into the society's culture. He believed that "man is man", (meaning that a person acquires human qualities) because he or she lives in a society. Durkheim also maintained that society is larger than the individual, that society is the totality of the individuals and it manifests itself through such things as beliefs, norms, value systems, knowledge, skills and traditions of people of a given society. Therefore, society continues to exist even when one of its members dies.

- To provide norms and values a child needs in order to fit in the society. For Durkheim, education was a means of organizing the individual self, or me and us (representing other people) into a stable and meaningful unity.
- Equip the child with knowledge and skills for earning a living.
- Create order and stability in the society for it is through education that proper conduct of behaviour is developed in the members of society.

Durkheim's contribution to education is immense. He was among the first scholars to analyse education from a sociological perspective. Durkheim's major works in the field of sociology of education were published in collections entitled *Moral Education; Evolution of Educational Thought and Education and Sociology*. In these works, he provided a definition of education and also outlined concerns of sociology. In the *Evolution of Educational Thought,* he described the history of education in France, combining ideas from some of his other works in a historical analysis of the institution of education. He emphasized that in every time and place, education is closely related to other institutions and current values and beliefs.

In his work on *Moral Education***,** Durkheim outlined his beliefs about the function of schools and their relationship to society. To him, moral values were the foundation of the social order and therefore, society had by all means to perpetuate them through its educational institutions. He viewed classrooms as "small societies" and agents of socialization. He emphasized the importance of discipline in the classroom. He contended that education and discipline were necessary if the society was to remain orderly. Individuals lacking in self-discipline, he asserted, were incapable of respecting the rights of others and they were likely to do harm to themselves. Durkheim strongly believed that lack of proper standards of behaviour would lead to chaos or "anomie" in society.

Karl Mannheim (1893 - 1947) a German sociologist, also advocated a sociological approach to education. He stayed in Britain as a refugee to escape Nazi totalitarianism of 1930's and 1940's. While in London, he became a lecturer of Sociology at the London School of Economics. In 1940, he was invited to be a part-time lecturer at the Institute of Education of London University, and in 1946, he was appointed to the Chair of Education.

Mannheim saw education as a means of social control. In his book *Man and Society,* Mannheim claimed that sociologists do not regard education solely as a means of realizing abstract ideals of culture, such as humanism or technical specialization but as part of the process of influencing men and women. He further observed that education can only be understood when we know for what society and for what social position the pupils are being educated. He strongly felt that we cannot educate in a vacuum and argued that we must diagnose the sort of society in which we live in order to be able to plan our educational programme for a new and better society. In his book *Diagnoses of Our Time* published in 1943, he attempted to demonstrate this. In order to avoid the extremes of laizze-faire (a state of no rules) and totalitarianism (a state of dictatorship), he favoured democratic rule. Democracy, a government of the people and for the people and by the people, gives members of the society an opportunity to participate in the matters of the state or society. The planned democracy that Mannheim envisaged meant that there would be a need for consensus of values.

Mannheim and Stewart (1962) saw the sociological approach to educational problems as one which could ultimately provide some positive aims in education as well as in helping to establish both content and method. They said that:

> The principal contribution of the sociological approach to the history and theory of education is to draw to the fact that neither educational aims nor educational techniques can be

conceived without a context, but rather that they, are to a very large extent, socially directed (Mannheim and Stewart, 1962).

John Dewey (1859-1952) an American scholar, is one of the more recent educationists whose ideas contributed to the development of sociology of education. Dewey's concern about education began to grow after observing how fast the simple community life structures in his time were changing due to industrial revolution. He noted that the main institutions entrusted with the child's education, the church and school, were often unable to cope with change. They were inadequate in preparing a child to meet the new social ways adopted by the changing society. It seemed to him that the growing child risked facing utter confusion as he walked into adulthood in the new society. For instance, he observed that there were tensions developing between village and town life of which both pupils and adult were unconscious. Thus, while the village child was close to the earth and was fully aware of the context of his daily and social life, the town child was making use of facilities like toilets in the house, water from taps, and manufactured goods which the child did not know how they were made. To avert this seeming breakdown in the child's nurturing, Dewey, through his experimental school at Chicago, hoped to recreate community life within the learning environment. The main purpose of the *ideal school* was to foster a social spirit of co-operation and mutual aid and to provide, within the classroom itself, the sort of living situation in which co-operation might be elicited.

To achieve this mission, Dewey realized that a close relationship between school and the individual homes of children and the general neighbourhood or community should be fostered. He viewed the school virtually as a *second home* for the child and maintained that for a school to serve as a *second home*; it had to have a real sense of community life where common interests were pursued. According to Dewey, the school was a community in miniature, a micro-society that both reflected the larger society outside and also sought, in the long, run to improve it.

He believed that social co-operation elicited by his envisaged *ideal school* would benefit a child's social life at home and in the neighbourhood. Hence, by offering this kind of social education to a growing child, the child would be able to stand on his or her own. Indeed, he emphasized that it is the social activity that really educates children as they participate in the life of the home, the village and the wider community.

Dewey's ideas were developed by his followers into what we usually call the *Project Method* of teaching, which is now widely used in schools all over the world. A project refers to a co-operative study of a "real life situation" by a class, or even by a whole school under the guidance of the teacher. A project aims to achieve a number of things. Firstly, it aims to bring children into real contact with the activities of the school neighbourhood. Secondly, it hopes to present children with "real life problems" which they would solve by thinking and working together. Finally, a project endeavours to develop further skills and new knowledge in school subjects while working at the project. Examples of projects, for a town or school might be "The town we live in", or "The industries of our town" while those of village schools might be "Farming" or "The occupations of our village". The project method of teaching ensures that various aspects of activities on a given topic are assigned to groups of children. Each group is expected to study their particular aspect of their assignment, and then write a report for presentation to the rest of the class. At the end, reports from all the groups are synthesised into one with the help of the teacher.

The project method has several advantages. First, it is likely to capture the enthusiasm of many children, stimulate their initiative and encourage the spirit of enquiry. Second, it is expected to help children learn how to plan and co-operate with each other and this is likely to form a good basis of social training. Third, the project approach brings children into close contact with the problems of real life that they may fail to do by studying "subjects" in school. Finally, the subjects of the curriculum are seen to be connected with real life outside the school. One of the disadvantages of the project method is that the needs of an individual may be neglected by the emphasis on social activity.

Educational Sociology and Sociology of Education

Educational sociology, now known as sociology of education, is a fairly recent field of study. It has been noted that the development of educational sociology has undergone several stages. The first stage in the study of educational sociology, which was referred to as *sociology of teachers*, began in 1900, and lasted up to 1910. During this phase, the discipline was not research based; it simply borrowed the findings of sociology and applied them to the institution of education for the purposes of training teachers. Thus, sociological literature and findings from the field of sociology deemed relevant to education were collected, edited and then termed as educational sociology. The second stage came in 1923 during which American scholars established *National Society for the Study of Educational Sociology*. This organization began to sponsor educational researchers. The establishment of the society was followed by the founding of the *Journal of Educational Sociology* by Payne and others in 1927. The journal became an important vehicle for disseminating knowledge on educational issues. It changed its name to *Journal of Sociology of Education* in 1928 (Angel, 1928). By this time, the study of educational sociology had become a recognized field of study. Later, authors interested in education published their works under Sociology of Education (Mannheim, and Stewart, 1962).

Educational sociology and sociology of education concern themselves with the institution of education. However, they have several distinct differences. According to Jensen (1965), educational sociology has the task of developing knowledge with relevancy to the problems of educational practice. Some of these may be concerned with the organisation of a learning situation for the attainment of educational objectives, formulation of learning objectives and identification of the most effective and efficient educational methods and technology for the accomplishment of the educational objectives. The teacher, for example, looks at educational sociology from the point of view of solving practical problems in relation to educational practice. On the other hand, sociology of education is concerned with investigating the sociological aspects of educational phenomenon and institutions.

Jensen (1965) asserts that the needs of educational practice are only incidental to the purposes of such sociological investigation. This kind of analysis strongly suggests that sociology of education is in the realm of sociologists. However, if the study of the relationship between education and society is to be meaningful, the sociologist and the educationist must work together. Thus, while of necessity education must apply the sociological perspective in dealing with practical aspects of education, the educationists must be involved in the sociological research so that they do not lag behind in the acquisition of new concepts and development of new theories. This approach is particularly relevant today since almost all universities worldwide teach sociology of education rather than educational sociology. It is, therefore, imperative to strike a balance between educational practice and sociological theories in the study of sociology of education. This combination will ensure that the recipient of sociology of education can handle competently, practical as well as theoretical issues related to the institution of education.

Concerns of Sociology of Education

Sociology of education is a scientific study of relations between society and the institution of education. In the study of the various relations between society and education, sociology of education systematically observes and analyses education with regard to its social use and significance in a particular society; its influence on society; the social relationships and organization in schools and classrooms; teachers and their relationship to pupils, parents and community at large. Other issues systematically observed and analysed are problems associated with the institution of education; relationships between various institutions of the society such as the family, government, the economy, the church and the various other organizations on education; the child's social environment and culture and their effects on learning. It further examines the role of the teacher in the educative process and also the teaching profession and its status in the society. It is expected that the study of the interrelationships of various social institutions with education such as the economy, the government, the family and religious organizations for instance and its interactions with other stakeholders will help teachers to understand the goals of education and variables that influence the educational process and outcomes.

Summary

The study of sociology of education is a recent phenomenon. Emile Durkheim was one of the first scholars who recommended the study of the relations between education and other social institutions at the beginning of the twentieth century. He viewed education as a "social thing". Thus, he defined it as an influence exercised by adult generations on those not yet ready for social life. Other scholars who highlighted the interrelationships between education and society included Karl Mannheim, and John Dewey.

The study of the relationship between education and society up to late 1920's was known as educational sociology. After this, it adopted the name *sociology* of education. The difference between the discipline of educational sociology and sociology of education was that the former was not research based; it simply borrowed the findings of the discipline of sociology and applied them to the institution of education. *Sociology of education,* on its part, applied the use of scientific methods to investigate and analyse the institution of education, including its interrelationships with other social institutions and their impact on the educational process and outcomes.

Study Questions

1. Discuss the contributions of Durkheim and Karl Mannheim towards the development of sociology of education.
2. Discuss the origins and development of sociology of education as a branch of sociology.

3. Evaluate the contribution of John Dewey's ideas towards the enhancement of community life inside and outside the school environment.

References

Angell, Robert. (1928). Science, Sociology and Education. *Journal of Educational Sociology, Vol.1* pp. 406 - 413.

Clarke, F. (1948). *Freedom in the Educative Society*. London: University of London Press.

Dewey, John. (1900). *The School and Society*, Chicago: University of Chicago Press.

Durkheim, Emile. (1922). *Education et Sociologie*, Paris.

Jensen, G. E. (1965). *Educational Sociology*. Center for Applied Research in Education: Prentice Hall.

Mannheim, K. (1940). *Man and Society. In an Age of Reconstruction*. Routledge.

Mannheim, K. (1962). *Diagnosis of Our Time Your Impression*. Routledge.

Mannheim, K. and Stewart, W.C. (1962). *An Introduction to the Sociology of Education*. London: Routledge.

Morrish, Ivor. (1972). *The sociology of Education: An Introduction*. London:George Allen & Uniwin.

Shimbori, Michiya. (1979). Sociology of Education *International Review of Education Vol. 25* P. 394.

3

Sociological Theories and their Application to Education

Definition of Sociological Theories

A sociological theory is defined as facts, ideas, and principles that attempt to explain the nature of society, its organizations, structures and patterns of behaviour. Principles of a theory guide observations and lay the foundation for sociological description. Sociological theories are generally referred to as sociological models because they explain how society or aspects of society work.

Sociological Theories of Education

The major sociological theories include structural functionalism /consensus, conflict, symbolic interaction, ethno methodology and feminism. Since education is one of the key institutions of society, these theories are used in analysing the content of education, its aims, teaching methodologies, and outcomes. Education sociologists utilize theories to a large extent to examine how groups influence individual learners and also the functions of the school in the society. These sociological models also try to explain the nature of the school and the kind of people who benefit most from the school programmes.

Structural-Functionalism/Consensus

Structural-Functionalism/Consensus is a theoretical orientation that emphasizes the functions or contributions made by individuals to society's existing social structures. The theory draws its explanatory power from the biological workings of an organism. Its premise is to explain how society is maintained in a state of consensus while avoiding conflict. The functionalists maintain that society is like a human body, with a specific structure, consisting of various institutions which function in harmony. The different parts of the body perform different functions which aim to satisfy the basic needs of the organism (functional prerequisites). Likewise, in society, each institution has a specific function (or functions) and the different institutions of society are dependent upon one another for various services. For example, education as an institution is connected in various ways to the economy, the family, and the political and religious institutions. Each social institution is a complex structure. Education system for example, is made up of different layers or sub-systems, namely: pre-unit, primary, secondary, tertiary, and university level of education. Each of these sub-systems has its own functions to perform within the organized whole. The different sub-systems are further made up of smaller units such as departments or classes, which in turn are composed of roles (Ezewu, 1984).

The propagators of this theory are Auguste Comte, Emile Durkheim, Herbert Spencer, and Talcott Parsons. Auguste Comte believed in social integration and emphasized the interrelatedness of the various parts of the society in the same way the different parts of the body relate to each other to produce a harmonious working of the body. The interrelatedness of the various societal parts work toward progress.

Emile Durkheim (1858 - 1917), an astute advocator of the functionalist theory, analysed suicidal cases during the industrial revolution in Europe. He looked at suicide not through the action and motivation of individual actors, but through the attributes of various social groups, forces and social context in which the action took place. Durkheim, like Comte, stressed the interrelatedness of social facts. Herbert Spencer, like biologists, likened society to a living organism whose parts must work together in order to sustain it. For example, the heart, brain, lungs, kidneys and all other parts of the body must work in harmony for the body to be in good health and to survive. Similarly, in society, the various institutions, such as the family, schools, religious organisations, and the like have to be co-ordinated for the society to function properly.

Talcott Parsons (1903-1979), an American scholar and one of the best known contemporary theorists of functionalism, articulated his ideas about the society in his book entitled *Social Structure and Personality,* published in 1964.

- He believed that society is held together by value consensus, that is, agreement regarding the goals of the system and the appropriate means of achieving these goals.
- He identified major sectors of the society as economics, politics, religion, education and the family. These sectors form social systems in terms of activities and functions of the society.
- He recommended role differentiation and assignment of such tasks to competent people to perform them.

The originators of the functionalist theory postulated that:

- Society is held together by value consensus, that is, agreement regarding the goals of a system and the means to achieve it. Without a harmonious social order, there would be conflict and discord. Therefore, this harmonious social order should be saved and passed from generation to generation;
- Every social structure of the society has a purpose;
- Social structures form social systems. Social systems refer to a set of persons or groups; these are dependent on each other. Each set of persons or groups is conceived as a social unit distinct from particular individuals who compose it;
- Various roles in a society should be assigned to qualified people to avoid the collapse of social structures or social systems. For example, teachers should have the knowledge and skills for the job. Likewise, doctors should have knowledge of medicine while bankers should be well equipped for the banking industry;
- Society should be bound by goals known to all and should guide all regardless of their social and economic status;

- Individuals should be well socialised into the culture of their particular society;
- An effective control of disruptive forms of behaviour such as corruption, tribalism, violence, and all other social vices must be put in place; and
- People must recognise legitimate authority, and thus obey laws willingly because they want order in society;

Functionalists claim that once the general function of an institution is known, then it is possible to trace the particular functions of its sub-systems. Within the sub-system, we can also discover the functions of the various components and how they relate to and complement one another. For example, once the function of education is established, it is then possible to understand how primary, secondary and tertiary levels of education contribute to the performance of this function. It is also easier to explain how the roles of head-teacher, classroom teacher and pupil are organized within any school so as to enable the school function effectively. If any part of society acts contrary to its functions, then dysfunction occurs. For instance, malfunctioning of primary education will create dysfunctions in the entire institution of education.

Implications of Functional Theory to Education

The relationship between the structure of society and the function of society is that education is seen as a sub-system of society. The system of education is analysed primarily in terms of the function it serves, that is, provision for the maintenance of social order, its legitimating, transmission and internalization of social values. Education, thus, is a socialization tool. This position to educational practice can be derived from the following perspective:

- Education, in a broad sense, is considered to be a conservative or an integrating force. It basically works towards solidarity and integration rather than towards differentiation and managed pluralism. Individuals are channelled to view social phenomena as one and the only side to a coin.
- This view about education influences the interpretation of three key areas of schools, that is, the curriculum, the role of the

teacher, the role of the pupil and how the teachers and pupils relate.

Regarding curriculum, an idea can only find its way into the school curriculum if it is part of the common collective nature (Blackledge and Hunt, 1985). A good example of this in Kenya was the controversy that surrounded the introduction of aspects of sex and family life education into the school curriculum. While those who championed the idea thought that aspects of sex education should be included in the curriculum to make school teaching relevant to changing times, those who opposed it held that discussing sexual matters between adults and children was not part of the African collective culture. The position of the functionalists, therefore was that education realised individuals in the manner society wished them to be, and not as nature made them.

The role of the teacher in a school setting is, therefore, to encourage group involvement among pupils, allegiance and responsibility. The teacher is expected to enable pupils to recognize that their allegiance to societal goals and values comes before personal or family concerns, and to develop in the pupil those skills which society needs in order to function and which the children will require in order to survive in society. The image of the ideal pupil derived from the functional theory is that of a passive being with restraint; who is selfless, self-disciplined, and cooperative; one who identifies with the common social good. However, to be properly socialized, the acceptance of common social values by the pupils must be based upon understanding, that is, to be derived from reasoned explanations.

While education aims at producing well-disciplined and cooperative individuals, it should also produce experts in various fields in society. Parsons (1959), perceived the school as a specialized agency that was expected to become the principal selection and socialization of the young in line with what they would be required to do in an increasingly differentiated and progressively more advanced society.

Criticism of the Functionalist Theory

1. It emphasizes the status quo and maintenance of order and eliminates conflict as a possible alternative to social order. In education, the theory implies that the effectiveness of any school structure can be measured only in form of the needs of the system. This view is not wholly right because consensus is only one way of maintaining social order. In other instances, social order is maintained by use of threats. The idea of pluralism in education, politics and in the economy is now being embraced as the best way of maintaining social stability by agreeing on checks and balances.

2. It reiterates a holistic view of the society at the expense of tracing historical development of certain social forces and effects. The theory provides a deterministic view of the relationship between individual and society. Society and culture are not seen as being shaped by individuals. Hence, a virtually important dimension of social life, that is, contribution of an individual to society, is ignored.

3. It is preoccupied with maintenance of social stability at the expense of innovation. Innovation is seen as a threat to the status quo. Thus, criticism is not welcomed; it is either suppressed or taken in piecemeal. Remedial measures are used to contain the problem.

4. Human beings are viewed as approval seekers. Any action by a person is seen to be motivated by the urge to seek approval and acceptance in society. However, whereas approval seeking is an important human motive, to interpret human motives only on the basis of approval seeking is to present an over-integrated view of society. For example, a student may do what is expected of him or her, not because the student wishes to avoid punishment or ridicule but he/she feels satisfied in doing the right thing. Similarly, a student may work hard and behave well, not because he or she is seeking approval, but because he/she enjoys the work, is interested in learning, and wants to proceed on with further education.

5. It makes an individual subservient to society. Society rather than its individuals in the society are said to have needs, motivations and requirements. An individual from this perspective is over socialised to the extent of being controlled by forces beyond his/her will. An individual is painted as having no control of his or her destiny.

Conflict Theory

Conflict theory is a theoretical orientation emphasizing opposition among individuals, groups or social structures. Fundamental to such opposition is the existence of scarcity or limitations on resources for achieving goals. The theory is different from structural-functionalism in that it tries to explain differences experienced by both individuals and groups in terms of their access to, and ability to use resources in society. Conflict can be defined as any action that obstructs, prevents, interferes or in some way makes one's activity less likely or less effective than another's. Conflict can originate in a person, intra-person group or intra-group. In general, Conflict Theory looks at the nature of resources different people and groups have at their disposal or under their direction. The resources include material benefits, wealth, privileges, status, and knowledge.

The main proponent of conflict theory is Karl Marx. He proclaimed that "the history of all existing society is history of class struggle" (Karabel and Halsey, 1977). For instance, there is struggle between those in power and the ruled, rich and poor, educated and uneducated, those who are economically powerful and the poor. He claimed that the structure of the industrial society is such that it breeds conflict in every stage.

Society's competing groups, i.e. the "haves and the have-nots" are seen as being in constant state of tension leading to the possibility of revolution. The "haves" often use coercive power and manipulation to hold society together, but change is inevitable. Sometimes, change is rapid as the conflicts of interest lead to the overthrow of an existing power structure.

Assumptions of Conflict Theory

Unlike the functionalists, conflict theorists view social order as being sectional struggles between those who wield power, and the ruled. In other words:

- Social life is a manifestation of conflicts between different social groups and classes. This is because values and norms are not the same for all members but vary according to one's position and self-interest. Interests are never identical for all except for those who share the same privileges;
- Social life involves coercion, persuasion, division and inequalities. Division in the society exists between the poor and the rich, rural and urban dwellers, high-cost versus low-cost schools, public universities versus private universities, men and women, people of different races and tribes. Thus, conflict theorists attribute the characteristics of coercion, division and hostility as well as change, to society itself. There is a marked emphasis on the significance of interests and power;
- Social differentiation involving power and political leadership is maintained through force;
- Social institutions are constantly changing and no amount of force will prevent change;
- Those with power influence every aspect of social structures including values and beliefs. Karl Marx maintained that educational systems perpetuate the existing social classes. The expansion of school program therefore is motivated by capitalists' desires to serve the needs of their own class, in terms of preparing future owners and managers of the capitalistic economic structures. Social class according to Karl Marx, refers to division of society into two distinct hierarchy of classes–the "haves" capitalists or owners of means of production, and the "have nots" or proletariats or labourers in the capitalistic economic system;
- The opposing groups to the status quo are coerced into accepting the existing power relations and social structures. Marx, however, argues that change is inevitable and sometimes it is

rapid thus leading to a revolution and the overthrow of the existing power structures.

Functions of Conflict Theory

This theory serves society in the following ways:

1) It prevents stagnation in society because the structure and norms of a group are gradually modified in the process of handling conflict.

2) It stimulates interest and curiosity. As people look for solutions to problems in the society, they discover new ideas and interests which in turn provoke curiosity into discovering more ideas and strategies in tackling social problems.

3) It is a medium through which problems can be aired and solutions arrived at, thus effectively preventing "open" war and social disintegration.

4) The process of dealing with a conflict brings about personal and social change. For instance, fight against corruption will change moral outlook of individuals and may improve transparency in the government.

5) Conflict within a group frequently helps to strengthen existing norms and also contributes to emergence of new forms. Social conflict is a mechanism of establishing a new social order or equilibrium. Conflict can neither be eliminated nor even suppressed for long.

Implications of Conflict Theory to Education

Conflict theorists view schooling not as a process of socialization, but rather as a process related profoundly to the distribution of resources and opportunities in societies. Education is seen to be influenced by the ideologies of socially and politically dominant groups in society. Thus, conflict theorists suggest the following:

1. Reform in education should be frequent and should be preceded by changes in the economy and in the political and social structures. Economy and power are viewed as the most powerful forces in society.

2. Education should be reviewed constantly to accommodate all interested groups and in order for it to bear desirable fruits. It should be worked upon by experts.
3. Performance of students in different categories of schools differs due to unequal allocation of resources, and not necessarily due to intellectual endowment and hard work.

Criticisms of the Conflict Theory

Conflict can divert away performance and goal attainment. Continued conflict can have a heavy toll on the psychological and social well being of people such as inhibiting group cohesiveness.

The theory overemphasizes the influence of economic determinism over other aspects of society. For example, it shows social change accruing from a conflict of economic interests, disregarding the influence of ideology and political power. It is important to note that individuals are not helpless victims of an economic system but also active agents. Therefore, institutions such as schools should be viewed not only as sites for the reproduction of economic inequality, but also sites for resistance and struggle.

Karl Marx overemphasized the economic class conflict and ignored the status-group conflict perspective. Max Weber, argued that an economic class is too narrow as a basis for determining individual or group status. In society, for example a church minister may have a higher social status than a rich man. These individuals represent interests of the people they lead and serve. According to status conflict position, it is conflict among these diverse statuses that explain how change in education and society occurs. Thus, school programmes may be incorporated in curriculum to serve interests of religious groups while others like computer studies may be included to serve the interests of communication and industry. For instance, in sexual matters, the Catholic Church has objected to the use of condoms as one of the ways of preventing AIDS infection during sexual contact. Instead, the church has recommended sexual abstinence until marriage and faithfulness to one's sexual partner in marriage.

Similarities and Differences between Conflict and Structural/Functional Theories

1. Both theories are concerned about society, social order, and they also try to analyse society in its totality.
2. Whereas conflict theory recognizes that there are tensions in society, the functional theory does not and emphasizes stability and social equilibrium.
3. Conflict theory would recommend constant review of social institutions while functional theory would tackle problems when they arise.
4. Conflict theory accommodates social change, functional theory prefers suppression of change.

Symbolic Interaction Theory

This theory focuses on an individual's definition of the situation, roles and self-image. Unlike functional and conflict theories, which focus on the society in its totality symbolic interaction theory focuses on the individual in the social context. The theory attempts to explain how humans form their self-concept and self-identity through the use of symbols and interaction with other people. According to interactionists, human beings become social beings when they are able to learn the attitudes and emotions with which objects, actions and behaviours are viewed by others.

The main proponent of this theory *George Herbert Mead (1963-1931)* argued that development of human behaviour is due to the functional language (that is, use of symbols) and the person's social interaction. The symbol and human being's ability to use the symbol in verbal communication are what develop human behaviour. Mead also alludes to two levels of communication: the non-symbolic communication (use of gestures) and symbolic communication (use of ideas and concepts). Thus, the transformation of an individual into a minded organism or "self" takes place through the agency of functional language.

The term symbolic interactionism incorporates two words, namely, symbols and interaction. Symbols are items or actions to which meaning is attached by members of the group. Language is the means by which symbols are created and transmitted in language form. Examples of symbols include a smile, a wink, a salute, a car, pen, book, chair and so on. Interaction refers to contact with others including our reactions to them. Symbols, therefore, communicate meaning and include vocal sounds and gestures. A good example of the latter is the sign language for the deaf. In a social interaction, therefore, when one uses symbols, an action that is appropriate to it is expected to take place.

The argument of the symbolic interaction theory is that all our actions have symbolic meaning. Under the symbolic interaction theory, there are two sub-theories that are useful in sociology of education. These are Labelling and Exchange theories.

Labelling Theory

This theory refers to categorization of people through labels on the basis of characteristics and the effects of such labels on people's behaviour and self-concept. A label is a term used to classify or describe persons according to various characteristics such as, clever, foolish, gentleman, and the like. A label can also be used to categorize people according to various ways of thinking (schools of thought) such as liberalism, authoritarianism, capitalism and many others. The label used on an individual may not necessarily describe the existing situation. However, with time, it is realised. The theory is a self-fulfilling prophecy even though it often begins with a false diagnosis.

A study by Rosenthal and Jacobson (1968), showed the effects labels have on people. Their findings showed that students behave well or badly depending on teacher expectations. For example, if a pupil is repeatedly referred to as clever and associated with leadership capabilities, the pupil can rise to position of leadership. The individual so described may incorporate the label clever and leader as part of his or her self-concept and behave as the labels suggest. Girls have for a long time been said to be "un mathematical". Since they are labelled that way, the outcome of poorer performance in mathematical subjects is used as "conclusive evidence" that the label is accurate and the explanation of a biologically situated difference is sound. Labelling is applied with most frequency. Therefore, because of labelling, girls believe they cannot perform well. Their performance then starts to deteriorate because of the poor self-concepts they have formed about themselves *(Meighan and Barton, 1978).*

Streaming in class based on ability is another form of labelling and it has detrimental effects on the performance of students. Kimokoti (1982), found out that although the government does not have a clear-cut policy on streaming in schools, streaming of pupils on the basis of their abilities in different subjects goes on. In some schools, pupils are streamed on how well they perform in a particular subject. For example, pupils who score between 90-100 marks in mathematics are put in the "A" stream, 79-89 marks in "B" stream, 59-69 in "C" stream and so forth. The pupils who perform below average according to the teachers' expectations are likely to be ignored. These pupils in turn internalize the label they are given and do not manifest much interest in academic subjects in which they are said to be weak. Such students then channel their energies to other activities such as sports while others drop out of school. Wanre (1994) in her study on streaming showed that pupils perceive themselves according to the streams they are placed, and perform according to the expectations of those streams. They internalize the label they are given and perform well and behave on the basis of that label.

This theory is important to education because it contributes to the understanding of mechanisms through which teachers come to hold certain expectations of the students, how they are operationalized and the overall repercussions of such expectations on students' performance and behaviour.

Exchange Theory

The theory is based on the assumption that there are rewards and costs involved in our interactions. It is, therefore, a theoretical orientation emphasizing goals and positive reinforcement associated with interaction. The exchange theory, like the labelling one, is a constituent of the symbolic interaction theory. According to this theory, interactions are expected to bind individuals and groups with obligations. For example, a student who learns well is rewarded by not only passing examinations, but also social recognition later on in life, while a student who refuses to learn can be discontinued from the education programme. On the other hand, teachers who perform well in their jobs are rewarded with salary increment and promotions. However, if a teacher does not take his or her job seriously, he or she can be dismissed from the job.

Thus, life is made enjoyable and meaningful by the rewards people receive for their actions. The main proponent of this theory is George Homans (1961). He distinguishes between psychic or intangible profits and material profits. He claims that we can improve our understanding why people do the things they do by shifting our emphasis from material costs and profits to psychic ones or non-material goals. The examples of these psychic goals include honesty, integrity, tolerance and dependability among others. These qualities create more lasting relationships. Examples of material rewards comprise money, land, and vehicles, while psychic rewards include, commendation, recognition and accomplishment of good academic results. Rewards and especially positive psychic ones and labels are important in shaping behaviour of individuals in and outside the classroom.

Value of Interaction Theory to Education

The symbolic interaction theory contributes greatly to the education system in several ways.

- It emphasizes that individuals are conscious beings acting and reacting to what is around them;
- It emphasizes observation as a method of study;
- It emphasizes that human behaviour is not static. It is continually changing in response to social and environmental demands;
- It views social life as a process rather than an equilibrium;
- It suggests that all social objects of study are interpreted by individuals and have social meanings;

- Our interactions with others partly make us who we are, and they give us identity and self-concept. Thus, by focussing on the study of the individual, the theory has great value on education since education aims to educate the individual for the benefit of the society;
- Rewards especially psychic ones and positive labels are important in shaping behaviour of an individual in and outside the classroom situation.

Weaknesses of the Symbolic Interaction Theory

First, the theory seems to examine human interaction in a vacuum of values. It does not show the source and nature of values which guide and direct human interaction. Due to lack of this, human interaction is treated as mere episodes without prior learned values and norms.

Second, the theory does not admit the presence of structural norms, which enhance standardized normative behaviour. In so doing, the theory does not adequately explain what motivates social members to behave in a particular way with a great degree of uniformity (Barton and Meighan, 1978).

Ethno-methodology Theory

Ethno-methodology theory is a theoretical orientation, which focuses on how definitions of the situation are constructed and how in turn they shape reality. Reality is seen as quite open to change depending on whether or not people continue to agree on the definition of the situation. This theory is associated with Harold Garfinkel, 1967. The term ethno-methodology liberally means methods that members of society employ to live in their daily activities. The world is seen as an ongoing series of activities and resulting accomplishments. Though people are viewed as rational, their approach to issues is guided by the demands of the situation. According to ethno-methodology orientation "practical reasoning, rather than formal logical is utilized in the managing and accomplishing of their everyday lives". The approach tries in a systematic way to describe the actions of people because they constitute part of individuals" social reality. The theory answers the question of how people, as actors, construct reality in practical terms and how they maintain the day-to-day ways of social life. It describes the ethnography of human interaction and their actions, and explains how any meaningful communication with other members of the society is achieved. Meaningful communication here refers to the language and other symbolic ways of communicating with each other. Therefore, the interpretation of social reality rests on people's everyday experiences. Their actions are part of social reality.

Unlike structural functionalist that focus on the forces that hold social structures together such as common goals or value consensus, ethno-methodologists focus on the forces that change them. Society, according to ethno-methodologist, exists only in the perception of members. Therefore, people themselves give social orderliness.

All human actions irrespective of who the performers are, provide in their perceptions their social reality and some order to the social system. The actions of people are dependent on situations and circumstances. For example, a student in a lecture hall listens to the teacher and takes notes and even shows respect to the teacher by being polite, respectful and obedient. The same student during the students' riot may stone the teacher's car. Each set of actions dictate how we respond. Human beings are always adjusting, manipulating, interpreting, ordering, explaining and accounting for our actions all the time. The actions and the meanings they carry are dynamic to change. The ethno-methodology approach therefore seems to imply that individuals are not cultural "dopes" doing whatever the society prescribes. The approach suggests strongly that individuals are active participants in the creation of individual self as well as social reality.

Feminist theories and education

Feminism is a doctrine or a social movement, which advocates the granting of the same social, political, and economic rights to women as the ones enjoyed by their male counterparts. The history of feminism can be traced back to the ideals of French revolution, which took place towards the end of eighteenth century. Even though women participated in the revolution, they did not gain the same social, political and economical rights as men. Deckard (1975) noted that women have had lower social status than men and that they have and are still being discriminated socially, economically and politically. She observed that the state of affairs is unjustified and it must be changed.

Generally, feminist sociologists have been concerned with differences in the educational achievements of boys and girls, liking for science and technological oriented subjects by boys compared to girls who seem to prefer humanities. The relationship between class, gender and race in the distribution of educational inequalities and reproduction and reinforcement by the school of the oppressive relationships perceived to be fostered by patriarchal male-dominated society. Within the feminist movement, there are three major ideological positions, namely: liberal, Marxist socialist and radical feminist.

Liberal Feminism

The adherents of liberal feminism argue that women should enjoy equal rights because all people are born equal irrespective of their gender, race, class and colour. Liberal feminism is thus committed to equal opportunities in education for all pupils irrespective of gender class and race. It is assumed that whenever inequalities are detected in the treatment of school pupils for instance, in the curriculum contents and in the subjects offered, these differences should be eliminated. Children should have access to the same schools, teachers, subjects, the same examinations, irrespective of race and gender. These are no good reasons, according to liberal feminists, why boys should not learn the subjects done by girls such as home science. Similarly, there is no reason why girls should not play football or do physics and perform as well as boys.

Differences in gender inequality of educational opportunities and other hidden discriminatory practices such as failure to pay attention to the needs of girls can be achieved through re-socialising society. According to liberal feminists, society stands to gain a lot by educating women who constitute more than fifty per cent of the human race. Their perspective is reformist in approach and has achieved some success in improvement of educational facilities for girls, and access to institutions that were only accessible to men. However, its pace is very slow. It has been noted that out of 917 million illiterates, two thirds are women (Ballara, 1992).

Marxist Socialist Feminism

Marxist socialist feminism perspective (theory) draws on Marxist theory to account for women's oppression and inequality in society. They link gender inequality to class inequality. They argue that schools exist to serve the needs of capitalism and to reproduce workers of a segregated labour force in the workplace. This in effect, is closely related to an unequal division of labour in the home. As a consequence, boys and girls are socialized and educated differently to fulfil different roles in a sexist and capitalist society.

Marxist socialist feminism contends that women did not always occupy an inferior place in the society. In the primitive society, the epoch of tribal collectivism, women were equals of men and recognised by men as such. In fact, they argue that during this period, women were cultural leaders because food gathering was more important than hunting. Hunting was done by men and was an unreliable source of food. The vegetable foods that women collected and prepared formed the staple food. Women also discovered agriculture and domesticated small animals thus making food more readily available. Although there was a sexual division of labour, women worked hard and they were respected for it. However, with emergence of capitalism towards the end of eighteenth century there came the diminished power and status of women in the society.

Socialist feminists, further give the institution of marriage (family) as a means of bringing women under the control of men. According to socialist feminists the family did not develop to fulfil human needs for companionship amply catered for by the communal clan, but its function was a preservation of wealth within the paternal line. The role of women within the family thus became that of a breeder especially of sons, to continue the family line and to inherit property.

In a capitalist economic set up, women join labour force at the lower ranks of the working class where the majority do the traditional service jobs. Since quite a number of women are less educated, they are hired for lowly paid jobs. Generally, many women are not wage earners and this makes them dependent on men for financial support. The economic vulnerability of women and especially in the family set up makes them fearful that if they do not toe the line their security and those of children will be jeopardized. Consequently, they exert a conservative influence on their children particularly girls and this helps in maintaining the status quo. The vision of socialist feminist of an ideal society is one where means of production would be publicly owned and the fruits of production equally distributed to all members of the society. In such a society, factors like sex, class, and race would no longer determine one's status or life style. Further division of labour along sex lines would disappear because functions related to rearing of children would be done by institutions set for that purpose, thus making it possible for women to engage in other life pursuits such as education, employment, and public life engagements.

Socialist feminists are criticized for assuming that all women belong to the working class. In addition, all women do not experience the same kind of oppression. For instance, black women may not be at par with female counterparts in multi-racial societies. Thus, while all women are discriminated against in the labour market, politics and education, black women may face more isolation and disadvantage in white-dominated societies.

Radical Feminism

Radical feminism is an ideological movement which attributes women's inferior standing in society and oppression to sex class system and patriarchy. According to Firestone (1970) the origin of sex class system lies in the biologically determined reproductive roles of men and women and therefore it predates all other forms of women oppression. Since women become pregnant and bear children, it is assumed that they are the natural nurturers. Thus, unlike the economic class which is society created, sex class is directly linked to biological reality which puts men into a more privileged position compared to women. As a result, reproductive differences between men and women led to the first division of labour whereby women stayed at home to take care of children and perform home maintenance chores while men worked outside home in order to provide for women and children materially. Effectively, women became domesticated into the private sphere whereas men occupied positions in the public sphere such as employment sector, government and leadership in almost all sectors of the society.

Radical feminists are convinced that oppression of women is mainly maintained by male instituted social structures namely: the family under patriarchy system, motherhood, love, sexual intimacy between men and women, and religion. These institutions, especially the family, boost up the psychological power of man at the expense of that of a woman. Besides being economically dependent on man, the woman is also without emotional independence and self-confidence. Her behaviour and actions, radical feminists argue, are geared towards pleasing men.

Radical feminists view patriarchy (system of government/social organization) as an elaborate system of male domination, for it gives men (fathers) right to exact obedience and to punish disobedience from members of the family particularly the wife. Patriarchy traces family descent from the male line rather than the female line. Most societies therefore, prefer male children to female ones in anticipation that they will carry on the family line. Women who do not beget sons are scorned upon even though biologically, a man is the determinant of the sex of a child.

Radical feminists advocate for the development of technology in the area of contraception in order to free women from giving birth throughout their procreative years which can begin at early teenage years to the age of fifty. They further suggest that babies should be reproduced artificially through test tubes. These measures would free women from the yoke of biology of child bearing and taking care of children. They further argue that oppression will not cease just because the biological determinants are overcome. They recommend that the social structures perceived to maintain and sustain male dominance be dismantled in order to free women from oppression.

As far as education is concerned, radical feminists contend that male power, which permeates the whole society is deeply ingrained in the practices and characteristics of schooling including the education system. In schools, the lessons taught and relationships that exist marginalize the education of girls. Boys for instance, study subjects that are more job-market oriented such as natural sciences and technology subjects while girls study humanity based subjects which lead to service jobs like teaching, catering, housekeeping, nursing and other service oriented jobs done by women. In the classroom, boys get more attention and encouragement from teachers than girls. This preferential treatment of boys enables them to acquire skills, knowledge and attitudes that enhance their power and consequent control of women in later life. On the other hand, girls learn to be docile and expect men to be leaders. To change this state of affairs, radical feminist advocate for a revolution and not reform in their fight against oppression of the female gender. Thus, Firestone (1970) maintained that oppression of women will be eliminated only when a new social order is established. The establishment of the new social order is dependent on the following:,

- Women must be freed from the tyranny of their reproductive biology. Child-rearing and even child bearing is expected to become the responsibility of society as a whole. Men as well as women will be involved. Advances in biological sciences should make use of artificial reproduction possible for those who wish to make use of it.
- The new social order should recognise full self-determination, of women and economic empowerment of both women and children.
- The total integration of women and children into all aspects of the larger society will be required.
- Sexual freedom must be guaranteed, thus people can live together as sexual partners in what radical feminists refer as "non-legal/companionate arrangement" without necessarily conforming to heterosexual relationships as long as those involved wish to be in such relationships.
- Abortion should also be legalised.

Criticism of radical feminism

The major weakness of radical feminism is that it is too confrontational and revolutionary, thus it has had little support from men.

Summary

Various sociological theories and their application to education indicate that some aspects of each of these theories operate within the institution of education. For instance, people in a community and even school are different and each has a variety of functions and roles to play. Conflicts are experienced now and again but consensus is sought for the purpose of running things smoothly.

Consensus theorists, for example, in a school system adopt the goal of promoting such norms as honesty, good citizenship and trust. If the school does not appear to attain such goals, the consensus theorists would then suggest corrective measures such as provision of counselling in an effort to reform students' behaviour.

Conflict theorists view inequalities in the school system and society as class struggles. The remedy to the problem therefore would be some basic changes in the basic economic or social structure. Symbolic interaction theorists, however, look at labels as ways and means of understanding individuals in their various set-ups, including the roles they play. Through interaction, we are able to relate to one another and develop meaningful relationship with each other.

All theorists view differently the issues of recruitment, achievement and placement in educational institutions. The consensus theorists emphasize ability as the key element that accounts for better performance in examinations, therefore, streaming or tracking of students according to their ability is justifiable. But conflict theorists argue that some students perform better because they have access to the right facilities while majority perform poorly because they are hampered by various factors such as inadequate educational facilities, and unqualified teachers, among others. Thus, those who perform better do so because they are in a favourable position and not necessarily being more intelligent.

Exchange and labelling theorists believe that rewards and punishments can be used in the modification of behaviour of students. The use of rewards(physical material), and particularly psychological rewards, help to motivate students to learn. Lastly, competitive spirit among students can be promoted and enhanced through group assignments.

All feminists, either liberal, Marxist socialist or radical agree that women, compared to their male counterparts, are oppressed and under-represented in all sectors of society. Nevertheless, they differ in their explanation of the causes for inequality and the strategies to eliminate the obstacles. While liberal feminists attribute women's disadvantages and oppression to socialisation process that undervalues women and also assigns them roles restricted to reproductive and domestic sphere, Marxist socialist feminists and radical feminists associate women's underprivileged positions to capitalism and patriarchal male-dominated social structures especially the family.

Similarly, their recommendations for the elimination of women's oppression are diverse. Liberal feminism advocate for re-socialisation of society and provision of equal opportunities while Marxist social feminists recommend establishment of social structures free from capitalism.

On the other hand, radical feminists demand abolition of all male dominated institutions and particularly marriage. A major contribution by feminist theorists is that they have made society aware of women's disadvantaged position in society. As a result of this advocacy, efforts are now being made towards elimination of inequalities between men and women in all areas of human endeavours.

Study Questions

1. The labelling theory defines a person as a certain kind of individual. It is evaluative and judgemental usually, though not always. Describe how this theory, affects a student's attitude towards learning, the learning outcome and self-image?
2. How does the Marxist critique of the school system view the role of the state in the achievement of educational goals?
3. The structural-functional theory emphasize cohesiveness of values in a given community or organization. Describe the role of the curriculum, the teacher and the student in promoting unity in the school set-up.
4. Using relevant examples, give a critique of different feminist perspectives in the understanding of the educational outcomes for both boys and girls.

References

Barton, L., and Meighan, R. (1978). *Sociology Interpretations of Schooling and Classrooms: A Reappraisal.* London: Driffield, Nafferton.

Blackledge, D., and Barry, H. (1985). *Sociology Interpretation of Education.* London: Croom Helm.

Blumer, Herbert. (1966) Sociological implications of the George herbert Mead. *American journal of Sociology.* March, University of Chicago press.

Burgess, R. G. (1986). *Sociology, Education and Schools: An Introduction to the Sociology of Education.* London: B.T. Bats Ford Ltd.

Ezewu, E., (1986). *An Introduction to Sociology of Education.* London: Longman.

Firestone, Sulamith. (1970). *The dialetic of sex.* NewYork: Bantain Books

Karabel, J., and Halsey A.H. (1977). *Power and Ideology in Education.* New York: Oxford University Press.

Kimokoti, A. C. (1982). *The Extent to which Streaming is Practised: A Survey Study of Nairobi Secondary Schools*. University of Nairobi: An Unpublished M. A. (Ed.) Thesis. Reid Ivan, (1978). *Sociological Perspectives on School and Education*. London: Open Books.

Olatunde, O., and Ade, A. (1985). *Sociology: An Introductory African Text*. London: Macmillan.

Schultz, T.W. (1961). Investment in Human Capital, *American Economic Review* vol 51, March, pp.1-17 reprinted in J. Karabel and A.H.Halsey (eds), *Power and Ideology in Education*. London Oxford University Press.

Wawire, V. (1994) *The Impact of Streaming on the Performance of Students: A Case Study of Chebuyusi Boys' Secondary School, Kakamega District, Kenya*. Kenyatta University: An Unpublished M. Ed. Thesis.

4

Socialization and Education

Meaning of Socialization

Socialization is the acquisition of social characteristics of a human being. It is the process through which individuals learn the culture of their society steadily so that they are able to live fully and function in it as responsible adult members (Ezewu, 1983:6). Human infants are not born with the ability or knowledge to participate in various activities in their own societies. They are completely helpless, unable to feed and clothe themselves. They therefore, seek protection from those around them.

Primary socialization, the most important form of socialization, takes place during infancy within the family. Through interaction with the family members, the child learns the language and many other basic behaviour patterns of the particular society. Every society has its own specific methods of teaching young ones its social ways. Thus,. socialization is very important because without it, an individual would bear little or no resemblance to any human behaviour defined as normal by a given society.

Process of Socialisation

Socialization is said to be a life-long process. For the process to be successful, especially in childhood years, the following are vital:

Timing

Socialization must be time-oriented. No individual is able to learn everything at once. For example, one cannot toilet train a one-day old infant, neither can we expect a standard one pupil to acquire the knowledge of calculus unless other skills such as reading and writing are taught first. We learn better as we mature physically and mentally, and we easily acquire more advanced skills after mastering simpler or basic knowledge. It is physical, mental maturity and mastery of skills that is thus time-bound. Therefore, timing is an important factor in the process of socialization. It ensures that we are at the appropriate stage where normal individuals are capable of learning and undertaking a specific task.

Sequence of Events

Socialization is characterized by a sequence of events which occur in stages during one's lifetime. These events are important because they prepare a child for the various roles in life. Freud (1950) identified five stages of socialization that all individuals pass through from infancy to adulthood. We, however, must bear in mind that there is no distinct boundary between one stage and the next. Thus, there is normally overlap of events of the previous stage into those of the next stage, as the events of a previous stage diminishes as those of the next stage become more prominent. For our purposes, we shall only discuss Freud's stages of social development even though Erikson (1978) expanded Freud's five stages of socialisation in to eight. These span from birth and to old age (see appendix 1). Freud's stages of social development are outlined hereunder.

Oral Stage- Birth to 18 months

This stage starts from birth to 18 months, which signifies the initial period of a baby's life. During this period, the baby depends only on the use of the mouth to communicate. The only audible language known to the baby is crying. The baby learns to signal need for care. At this stage, the parent must try to figure out what the crying signals mean and respond accordingly.

Anal Stage

At this stage, the child learns how to control bowel movements, learns to receive and give love. Through repeated cues, cautions, rewards and punishments given by the parent or other care providers, the child begins to avoid some incorrect behaviour such as wetting, breaking things, telling lies and rudeness. Here, the child slowly becomes aware of oneself as a separate being from the mother and realizes that certain specific activities are performed by the parent, for example, the preparation of meals by the mother. At this stage, the parent (particularly the mother) performs the role of a socializer on behalf of the society.

Oedipus Conflict/Phallic Stage

This is the stage from three to six years old. The oedipal period is marked by a crisis called the "Oedipal Crisis" during which the child realises, that he is being cared for by a lot more people in the family than the mother alone. The child not only learns to identify, accept and trust other members of the family but he also learns to interact with them. Through interaction with family members, the child first learns to be a full member of the family and, then, to interact with other people in the wider society. If the child is restricted from learning this social interaction at this early stage, the child may become a social misfit.

A feature that appears prominently at this stage is jealousy. This feeling arises from the children's tendency to become closely attached to the parent of the opposite sex. Thus, a boy will tend to show greater attachment to the mother and thereby display a feeling of jealousy towards the father who may appear to be in competition for the mother's attention. Freud termed this feeling of jealousy in the boy the *Oedipus complex*. The *Electra complex* is the strong attachment the girl has for the father and the feeling of jealousy she displays towards the mother who is seen as a competing factor in the father-daughter relationship.

But as the children grow, certain social measures are taken to mould the child into an individual that reflect the appropriate sex role. In the western society children are given toys that reflect their separate roles. In the traditional African set up, children are taught activities that reflect their expected sex role. Boys for example, will imitate their fathers in looking after cattle, while girls assist mothers in baby-sitting, fetching firewood, water, cooking and housework chores. It is hoped that once a boy or a girl has learnt to identify certain tasks and activities considered appropriate for his/her sex, he/she will look upon the father or mother as the model and therefore make the correct sex role identification. Sex role orientation starts seriously at the age of six years.

This is about the period when formal schooling begins. In school, therefore, a child must learn to obey rules and play the games of the peer group. The child must learn to share, be responsible, honest and cooperative if he/she wants the friendship to continue. The school tasks must be learned in accordance with what the society expects of its grown-up members.

Latency Stage

Once the oedipal conflict has been resolved the child enters a period of latency from about six years to puberty or adolescent stage around the age of eleven years. Throughout this period, the child's sexual feelings are "latent". They are busy exploring the world and learning new things.

Adolescence Stage

This stage is the dawn of adulthood. It begins with the onset of puberty and includes the years we normally refer to as the teen years, that is, roughly between twelve and nineteen years of age. It is the intervening period between childhood and adulthood.

Adolescence period is characterized by crisis, conflicts and disagreements between parents and adolescents. The adolescents start to demand independence from parental control in order to be free to experiment with certain activities such as sex and other forms of hidden behaviour such as drug taking. During this stage, adolescents undergo important body maturing processes such as sex maturity which drive them to desire sexual intimacy. Other characteristics of the adolescents include evolvement of their own language code so that parents cannot get to understand them. For example, in urban towns like Nairobi, the sheng' language (a mixture of English, Swahili and some vernacular languages) is unique to youngsters. Through this language, youngsters have formed their own peculiar culture. But as much as adolescents want freedom, parents have a duty to control them from participating in activities that are not in line with the morals of the society. To come out of this stage successfully, adolescents require a lot of counselling and guidance from their parents, teachers and the responsible members of the society particularly in the management of sexuality. Many adolescent girls have become pregnant while others have contracted sexually transmitted diseases including AIDS because they are un-informed about dangers of sexual involvement and the precautions they can take to avoid such diseases.

Socialization as a life-long process that begins at birth and ends with death, occurs in many ways and at all times. Throughout life, individuals are constantly fitting their behaviour to social expectations. In a nutshell, socialization is the acquisition of culture of one's society or social group.

Socialization as a social learning process is best accomplished when there is the right kind of socially interacting parties. In other words, for socialization to occur there must be *socializees, socializers* and *definite environments*. Socializees, for example, may be a newborn baby, a new employee and so on. Socializers on the other hand, are the suitable persons to teach socializees. They include parents, teachers, peers, among others. Socializees and socializers interact not in a vacuum but in a definite environment so that through this interaction, the desired kind of socialization will be achieved. Thus the environment can be the family set up, the school environment and even place of work.

Agents of Socialization

For socialization to be achieved, a society uses a number of social structures within which a child is socialized. These socializing structures are what we shall refer to as socializing agents. It is within these various agents of socialization that individuals learn and internalise skills that are expected of them by society in their different stages of life.

The main agents of socialization are family, school, peer group, religious organizations, and mass media. Other structures in the society that may at times play the roles of socializing agents include clubs (both in schools and work places), associations, organized groups and the community itself.

The Family

The family is often referred to as the primary socializing agent. It is within the family that the child learns the first lessons in social roles, social behaviour, language and the general way of life of the society. Basically, the family is responsible for status socialization. This type of socialization tells members of the society who they are in relation to others in the community and the behaviour expected of them. For instance, in African traditional societies, children were expected to obey their parents, while the young were bound to respect old people. There are various categories of the family. They include the nuclear family-consisting of the father, mother and children. This is the predominant family in the western world although it is now practised in Africa especially by professionals. The extended family is the most common in Africa and Asia. In addition to the nuclear family, there are grandparents, cousins, sisters and in-laws.

The polygamous family, which is widely practised in Africa, is the marriage of more than one wife by one husband. In the western world this "marriage" is carried out secretly in the form of a husband keeping a mistress somewhere without necessarily the knowledge of the legal wife. Although polygamy is more common than polyandry, that is, where one woman is married to more than one husband, polyandry is nonetheless practised by a few people - a majority of them living in South Asia - Tibet, Nepal, India and Sri Lanka. India's polyandrous groups, known as the Phahris, live in the lower ranges of the Himalayas in Northern India (Kottak, 1991:328). Today, single parent family is prevalent the world over. It has increased with the escalation of high divorce rates especially in Europe and America.

Also, some of the economically empowered women are opting for families as single parents.

As a primary socializing agent, the family's major educational function is to initiate children into the cultural heritage of its society and in some way, that of the nation. Through the family, a child learns some patterns of behaviour, and acquires habits of thinking, which are features of the family and the wider society. In this way, the family, whether a nucleus one, polygamous or single parent family teaches the child the culture and sub-culture to which the child belongs (Odetola and Ademola, 1985). If a child is born in an agriculturalist family, the child will behave differently from one born into a pastoralist family. This is because the activities and even mode of thinking of the two families are quite different. Similarly, a child born in a Muslim family learns to behave differently from one born into a Christian family.

It is also in the family circle that gender roles are first introduced. From a very early age, children are either directly or subtly socialized into what the society expects of them according to their sex. Girls for instance, are given toys that relate to woman or mother activities such as cooking, baby-sitting, fetching of water, firewood and other general household chores. Boys on the other hand, are introduced to man or father roles such as looking after cattle and construction of houses among others. As the children grow up therefore, they pursue roles according to their sex depending on their culture and even religious beliefs. However, most learning that goes on in a family is informal. It occurs without the parents or other members of the family being consciously aware that they are teaching. As the children grow up, they join the school which is the next agent of socialization.

The School

The school is next to the family in terms to importance as agents of socialization. As the child enters school, she starts another long period of socialization level. During this time, the school shares the role of socializer of the child with the family. While the family does its socializing in an informal way, the school uses both formal and informal approaches in its socializing function.

The school curriculum provides the child with the formal knowledge of the basic intellectual skills such as reading, writing, verbal expression, quantitative and other cognitive abilities. Further, it allows the child to learn about history, technology and other areas of knowledge pertaining to the cultural achievement of the society. Additionally, the school provides the socializee with opportunities to acquire the social and vocational abilities which are necessary in order to make him a socially acceptable and economically productive member of the society.

Through textbooks the curriculum also socializes pupils into what the society perceives as suitable roles according to gender. One finds that most textbooks portray females as nurses, air- hostesses, teachers and workers at home, while males are portrayed as doctors, engineers, managers and state leaders such as presidents (Oburu, 1991). Consciously or unconsciously, the school has formally and systematically designated roles for pupils in their adulthood. For example, they learn how to behave towards their playmates and adults.

The child also learns how to share things and ideas, compete responsibly, cooperate, relate well and obey rules within his/her age group. Learning these values enables children to become respectful to those older than them, their acquaintances, and also internalize the culture of their wider society, and assist in their overall development as responsible members of the society.

The school environment enables it to fulfil its role as a socializing agent and thus benefit the socializee accordingly. For example, the adult teachers provide the child with the required formal learning. They also train the children according to the needs of the adult world. Since the children come from different families, socio-economic backgrounds and neighbourhoods, they represent variety of views, interests, expressions, habits and influences which are exchanged amongst children. The work of the school therefore is to intercept and change or modify those aspects which may not be acceptable to the community. Most of the informal learning occurs mainly within the peer group setting. The peer groups affect the socialization process both in school and in the neighbourhood.

The Peer Group(s)

Generally, a peer group refers to people of the same group. In school, normally, children in the same class form peer groups. In their classroom, children continually interact with each other as equals. This equality helps them to identify with the classroom group which is an important feature of peer group, socialization in school. Peer group is a recognizable agent of socialization among growing children as well as adults. Its influence on the individual is quite powerful and it can either be positive or negative.

In a peer group, the child learns values such as cooperation, responsibility, honesty and other good habits. These values are learnt through games and role acting. The children imitate the roles of husband and wife and thus learn responsibility. These values eventually become the basis of adult behaviour. Besides, the peer group helps children to learn the different sex roles and also acts as a source of information for its members.

Though peer group teaches what the society values, it can also influence somebody negatively. For example, smoking, drunkenness, drug-taking and immorality are vices that society teaches against. If therefore a child associates with members of a peer group that practise such things, the child's behaviour will be badly affected. Adolescence is a critical stage in the growing up process whereby this negative influences of socialization can easily occur (Meighan, 1981). It can conclusively be said that peer group influences children's behaviour thereby reinforcing the family and the school in their socializing roles in the society.

The Mass Media

The mass media includes radio, television, films, magazines and newspapers. Communication and entertainment are important facets of the mass media. All of these can help socialize individuals either positively or negatively just like the peer group. In the present world, the mass media has assumed a great role in the socialization of people and more so that of children. For instance, children are now more aware of the world and national affairs than those children of twenty to thirty years ago. They learn through the mass media certain manners, attitudes, behaviours and values that exist not only in their society but also worldwide. Knowledge on new issues such as farming, diseases, social life, languages among others is acquired. In this way, children become aware of new information and also get socialized through what they hear and see.

Research has shown that many young and old people who spend a lot of time watching television, get addicted and this sometimes results in negative socialization. Some of the problems caused by television watching–addiction include poor performance at school, reduced family interaction, loneliness, isolation, and laziness. Television watching also exposes some people to unacceptable activities such as murder, violence and unwarranted sexual behaviours. Liebert and Baron (1971) in their research study exposed a group of subjects to a TV production of an extremely violent cops-and-robbers type of programme. In a control led-condition, a similar group of children were exposed to a TV production of a highly action oriented sporting event for the same length of time. The children were then allowed to play together in one room. Those who had watched the violent TV programme showed more aggression against the other children who had watched the sporting event.

Books and magazines also have their negative and positive socialization. This means that if what is written is anti-social, the reader is likely to acquire similar behaviours. For example, though most romance novels make absorbing reading, they do not always teach the whole perspective of love and marriage; they always portray a couple blissfully marrying and living happily ever after, which is often not the case. By reading such novels, youths and even adults socialize themselves by imitating the characters portrayed and imagine their romance and marriage life to be the same. It is imperative therefore, that individuals be selective in what they watch and read for their socialization to be positive and meaningful.

Mass media has its positive effects in spite of negative influences on people. The new technologies in the media industry such as computers, and satellite communications systems have tremendously increased instant access to information. This has improved individual's ability to keep abreast with what is going on around the world. Thus, to such new technologies without access people would be disadvantaged as they would not be aware of the social change or trends taking place in other parts of the world.

Religious Organizations

The role of religious organizations in the socialization process is usually to perpetuate the morals, beliefs and practices of respective religious groups. The major function of religious organizations is to teach moral or good behaviour to children. This may be done by parents, teachers or those charged with the responsibility in their different religious organizations.

The acceptable behaviour teachings taught include respect of other people, obedience to parents, teachers and God. The adult, and especially the religious leaders, have failed to propagate good morals in society by not setting good examples. If religion is to make any positive impact on socialisation of children, religious leaders must practise what they preach. In addition, religious institutions must complement the efforts of the family, school and community in cultivating values in the youth. It should be acknowledged that religious teachings do not cover all aspects of social life. Therefore, education systems need to incorporate in their school curricula, subjects that teach about social ethics, moral values, family life and society's cultural values.

Socialization and Education

Socialization and education are both life-long processes. It is important to note that they are not synonymous. Socialization equips one with the acceptable norms of the society, where an individual is expected to absorb society's ways of life without questioning. Education, on the other hand, has the element of training and often follows a prepared curriculum designed to equip the individual with specific occupational skills, attitudes and knowledge necessary for earning a living. In addition, education teaches an individual how to think, to solve problems, to be rational and to distinguish logical and irrational thinking. Education helps one to make judgements and distinctions (Bennaars, 1993:4). Education, therefore, unlike socialization, can help an individual nurture and cultivate thinking ability.

Summary

From the discussion in this chapter, it can be stated that socialization is a life long process that starts with birth and ends at one's death. Socialization takes place as individuals mature into different stages of life and as they engage in various activities.

For socialization to be effective, agents of socialization play a vital role. For example, parents and other siblings enable the family to be a primary socializing agent. In the school, the curriculum content, teachers and peer groups are important features of the school as a socializing agent.

Socialization can be both positive and negative. This depends on the agent and the environment in which that particular socialization is taking place. For instance, it has been observed that the mass media is both educative and amusing. The amusement part, however, is sometimes negative and is thus, quite detrimental to an individual's socialization. This is especially true when such vices as immorality, violence, drug-taking and alcoholism are portrayed as acceptable societal norms.

Study questions

1. The school is said to be next to the family as far as socialization is concerned. Describe the features of the school in the formal socialization of children and youths.

2. What is the difference between socialization and education?

References

Barrow, Ribins & Milburn, Geoffrey. (1990). *A Critical Dictionary of Educational Concepts.* New York: Harvested Wheatsheaf.

Bennaars, G.A.. (1993). *Ethnics, Education and Development: An Introductory Text for Students on Colleges and Universities.* Nairobi: East African Educational Publishers.

Dalta, A. (1984). *Education and Society: A Sociology of African Education,* London: MacMilllan Publishers.

Erickson, Erik. ed (1978). Adulthood. New York: Norton.

Ezewu, E. (1983). *Sociology of Education*, London:Longman.

Freud, S. (1950). *The Ego and Id.* London: Hogarth press.

Bennaars, G.A. (1993). *Ethics, Education and Development: An Introductory Text for Students in Colleges and Universities,* Nairobi: East African Educational Publishers.

Haralambos, M. (1980). *Sociological Themes and Perspectives*, New York: Oxford University Press.

Liebert, R., and Baron, R. (1972). Some immediate Effects of Televised Violence on Children`s Behaviour, *Developmental psychology, 6*

Meighan, R. (1981). *A Sociology of Education*, London: Holt, Rinelta and Winston.

Olatunde & O. etial. (1985). *Sociology: An Introductory African Text,* London: MacMillan.

Obura, A. O. (1991). Changing Images, Portrayal of Girls and Women in Kenyan Textbook Nairobi: Acts press

5

Role and Purpose of Indigenous Education

The Concept of African Indigenous Education

Before the coming of the Arabs and the Europeans to Africa, the African peoples had developed their own systems of education. The view that Africans had no history and never taught their young ones anything was a mistaken belief of the Europeans. African children were taught both informally and formally in their communities.

Many scholars assumed that since Africans had neither reading nor writing skills, they had no system of education. To such scholars, education in Africa meant western civilization. These western scholars ignored anything traditional because of their restricted view of nature of education. To define education in terms of school or reading and writing is definitely fallacious. Schooling and education are not synonymous. Education should be looked as the `whole process by which one generation transmits its culture to the succeeding generation or as a process by which people are prepared to live effectively and efficiently in their environment. From these perspectives, it is quite clear that before the coming of the Europeans, there was an effective education system in each African clan, or chiefdom or kingdom. Sifuna and Otiende (1994:129) observed that African traditional education is as old as the evolution of the African race and that it was neither elusive nor visionary. It was effective, tangible, definite and clearly intelligible.

Education includes every process, except the genetic one that helps to form a person's mind, character or physical features. As a life-long process, it involves learning new ways of thinking and actions causing major changes in our lives. Essentially, education is the inculcation in each generation of certain knowledge, skills and attitudes by means of institutions such as rites of passage in traditional societies and schools in modern societies that have been deliberately created for that purpose. Education, therefore, belongs to the process known as *enculturation*, whereby selected aspects of cultural heritage are passed on to the growing person.

Education can be looked at from two points of view – the formal and informal. Formal education takes place in schools while informal takes place outside schools. Some aspects of indigenous education include child-rearing practices that are carried out primarily by the family and the community that the child and family belong.

There was and still is no single form of indigenous education in Africa. Societies developed different systems of education for transmitting their particular knowledge and skills. However, they were no great variations. It has been observed that indigenous forms of education had some remarkable similarities and one form in a particular society or tribe could be seen to have influenced another.

Goals of African Indigenous Education

Although indigenous education systems varied from one society to another, the goals of these systems were often similar. Indigenous education was essentially for the living and its main purpose was to train the youth for adulthood within society. Emphasis was placed on normative and expressive goals. Normative goals were concerned with instilling the accepted standards and beliefs governing correct behaviour. Expressive goals, however, were for creating unity and consensus. Although competitive elements within the education system were encouraged in intellectual and practical matters, they were controlled and subordinated to normative and expressive aims (Brown and Hisket, 1975).

What was taught related to the social life of the people concerned. Indigenous African education was not only concerned with the systematic socialization of the young generation into norms, religious moral beliefs and collective opinions of the wider society but also placed a very strong emphasis on learning practical skills and knowledge which was useful to the individual and the society as a whole. Essentially, indigenous education emphasized social responsibility, job orientation, political participation, spiritual and moral values.

The Curriculum

The term curriculum refers to a persisted course of study. The success of any education system depends on the nature of its aims and its curriculum content. From the physical environment, children had to learn about the weather, the types of landscapes as well as their associated animal and insect life. Additionally, they had to learn the people's attitudes towards the environments. They were also required to make proper adjustment to the physical environment by means of using equipment such as the hoe and axe, among others. In other words, children were taught how to cope with the environment, how to farm, how to hunt, how to prepare food, build houses and even how to run a home.

The curriculum envisaged the role of children in economic activities in their education and training. Parents and older relatives were responsible for their training in economic responsibilities. Learning by imitation played a big part as the smaller children followed the example of the older members in building, herding and hunting, in the case of boys, or sweeping, carrying wood, fetching water, and cooking, in the case of girls. Children were also taught their roles in the all-embracing network of kinship relationships and what their rights and obligations were in the society. Above all, every person in the homestead, as well as the community, knew his or her economic role and performed it with zeal both at individual and community level (Kenyatta, 1938).

Fundamentals of Sociology of Education

Methods of Instruction

In indigenous education, parents played a very important role in the education of children. Mothers educated all children in the early years, but later fathers took over the education of the male children while the mother remained in control of the females. Although there was overlap of roles of parents in tasks of training boys and girls before the age of six, the general rule was that of establishing sexual dichotomy in most work activities in order to prevent girls from becoming `mannish' and boys `womanish' (Sifuna and Otiende, 1994:135).

Traditional educators used various methods of instruction to attain the educational or learning purpose desired. These methods can be broadly divided into informal and formal. The informal method of instruction included learning through play, oral literature, dance, folk-songs and proverbs. Proverbs were used to convey precise moral lessons, warnings and advice to children. These had greater impact on the mind of the children than ordinary words.

As soon as children acquired communication skills at the age of about two years, they were made to conform to the morals, customs and standards of behaviour inherent in the culture of their society. Bad habits and undesirable behaviour, in form of disobedience, cruelty, selfishness, bullying, aggressiveness, temper tantrums, thefts and telling lies were not tolerated. Verbal warnings and corporal punishment were also used to enforce discipline.

Informal methods of instruction also involved subjecting children to work activities. Learning through the medium of work enabled children to acquire the desired type of masculine or feminine roles. Children learnt by doing and working hand-in-hand with adults. This kind of learning prepared children for their future roles as husbands and wives. Thus, of all the different aspects of educational training, which children were subjected to, the one to which most attention was paid was that which prepared them as prospective wives and husbands.

Formal methods of instruction involved theoretical and practical learning of skills. Learning through apprenticeship, for example, was formal and direct. Parents, who wanted their children to acquire some occupational training normally sent their children to work with craftsmen such as potters, blacksmiths and basket makers. The same was true with the acquisition of hereditary occupations. For example, a herbalist, in handing over his trade secrets (about which medicine to use for what disease), would instruct his child from time to time until he became knowledgeable and proficient in the practice.

Formal instructions were also given in the constant corrections and warning to children. These included some aspects of domestic work cultivation, herding, teaching children the customs and manners of eating, how to behave towards relatives and different people of varying ages, preparation for marriage, and handling parental and marital obligations.

Among some ethnic groups, formal education took the form of succeeding stages of initiation from one status to another. The most prominent of initiation practices were those associated with puberty which took the form of circumcision. Circumcision was regarded as the point of passage into full membership of the community. It was deliberately made an emotional and painful experience, (sometimes covering a period of many months) which was engraved forever on the personality of the initiates. Without circumcision a man could not be regarded to be a full member of the ethnic group or have rights of property. Circumcision was normally accompanied with formal lessons on how to behave as an adult of a given community (Ole Sankan, 1971). Today, this rite and especially for females, is outlawed and regarded as genital mutilation and a violation of human rights.

Decline of Indigenous Education

Indigenous education in its pure form is not visible anywhere in Africa. The modifications, which it has been undergoing, have affected it very variedly depending on ethnic groups, religion, family and individual backgrounds. However, indigenous education still exists in modified forms. Thus, it is possible to find some elements of traditional African education in most Africans communities.

The traditional education system is not breaking up uniformly but in stages and by institutions. For instance, the initiation institutions seem to be quite fragile now. The institutions have become isolated practices, stripped of ritual and education underpinnings. The urban setting in Africa also threatens traditional education sustenance. In towns, the decline of the role of the family in sustaining cultural values is evident.

Indigenous Education Versus Western Education

Indigenous education was very effective during the pre-colonial period. Today, this kind of education is ignored and assumed to be irrelevant in a modern world. Traditional education has its weakness and deficiencies which make it inadequate for modern societal needs. For example, its attention was focused on the group, the clan and the tribe, which led to the neglect of the individual. Secondly, its adherence to tradition was an obvious hindrance to development. It served a static society with little change from generation to generation. It was not an education for change but it aimed at maintaining the status quo. Modern society, on the other hand, is very dynamic and today's societies must have an education that accommodates change and development of individuals. Unfortunately, indigenous education unconsciously and consciously suppressed the individual to standard norms accepted by a particular society.

Another drawback of indigenous education was that it did not teach numeracy and literacy skills. Such a system lacked permanence and a future. The development of external trade coupled, with the existence of governments, called for a system of written records. Lack of written records has led to disappearance of history of traditional societies.

Despite some of its weakness, traditional education still has an important bearing to the modern school. Indigenous education and western forms of education cannot necessarily be seen as opposing each other since there are ways in which they supplement each other. For example, traditional education was deeply rooted in the environment, both physical and social. It involved children in real life situations. In this area, modern education can borrow a leaf, that is, the importance of realism in education.

Indigenous education was guided by the principle of learning by doing. Children received functional learning which largely prepared them to live and work on the land as well as specialised occupations. An important implication to school curricula from this aspect of traditional education is that education should be work-oriented. Some other aspects of traditional education, which have been incorporated in modern schooling and should not be subdued, include values, folktales, dances and songs, play activities and oral literature.

Summary

From the discussion in this chapter, it is clear that both indigenous education and modern education have important roles to play not only to individuals but to the wider community as well. For instance, strong points of indigenous system of education can be used to complement modern education and social values where applicable. In this regard, the views, opinions and assessments of past and contemporary African educationists, who through research and experience have become aware of the value and goals of the various African societies, must be respected. Needless to say, those positive aspects of the African Indigenous education should be fused with the modern school curriculum.

Study Questions

1. Using examples, discuss the major differences between indigenous and western types of education.

2. Is indigenous education still relevant in Kenya today? Explain your answer.

3. Through interviewing old people in your community and studying materials from books and the archives, explain how the incoming generation was socialised into responsible adults before the introduction of the western type of education.

References

Hiskett, M. and Brown, G. N. (Ed.), (1979). *Conflict and Harmony in Education in Tropical Africa,* London: George Allen and Unwin Ltd.

Ole, Sankan, S. S. (1971). *The Maasai,* Nairobi: East African Literature Bureau.

Kenyatta, J. (1938). *Facing Mount Kenya,* London: Seckar and Warburg.

Sifuna, D. and Otiende, J. (1994). *An Introduction to History of Education,* Nairobi: University of Nairobi Press.

6

Moral Education Among African Indigenous Societies in Pre-colonial Era

Concepts of Morality and Moral Education

Morality is concerned with what is considered right and wrong. It refers to any set of norms or standards that guide and regulate the conduct of human beings living together in a given society. Lack of such standards leads to social disorder or anomie. Given that human beings are born neither moral nor immoral, the society is therefore charged with the responsibility of transmitting what is considered to be right and wrong to the new members of the society. In this chapter, we examine how African traditional societies in the absence of formal education or schooling used to teach moral education to new generations.

Definition of Moral Education

The term moral education incorporates two words, namely, moral and education. The word moral is derived from a Latin word *mores* which refers to customs, beliefs, values, norms and traditions of a particular society or community. *Mores* of a given community define morality of a given society in terms of what are regarded right or wrong, moral or immoral actions, thoughts and feelings. People in a society are obliged to abide with a particular society's mores in order to promote harmonious co-existence. The term moral therefore describes what is considered right or virtuous or wrong and evil in a given society. The term education too is derived from a Latin word *educare*. In ancient Rome, the verb *educare* used to refer to the general process of bringing up children in the community's or society's way of life or culture. International Dictionary of Education (1977:94) defines culture as the total values, beliefs, customs, arts, scholarship, institutions and artefacts of a group or nation.

By living and participating in a culture, the immature human being becomes a recipient of and a participant in a culture. Many social agencies, such as the family, the peer group, religious institutions, schools, media, and the state are involved in the process of enculturation.

The concept of education shows that it is wider than the aspect of moral education. While education refers to the entire process of passing on the cultural heritage comprising of knowledge, skills and moral values to the incoming generations, moral education focuses on what is considered right and wrong, that is, set of norms or standards that guide and regulate the behaviour of human beings living together in a particular society.

Moral education is specific to a particular society; hence, we are able to talk of moral education among African traditional societies. Traditional African societies can be described as black people who occupied Africa before colonization in the eighteenth and nineteenth century.

The African people, who belonged to various communities or societies, were characterised by their ethnicity, common language, beliefs, customs and traditions. For example, the Kikuyu, the Masaai, the Luo, the Kamba of Kenya, the Baganda and Acholi of Uganda, the Tutsis of Rwanda, the Yoruba of Nigeria and the Zulus of South Africa formed distinct societies and had their own set of moral standards. However, in spite of these societies having distinct characteristics, they had more or less similar goals with regard to moral education.

Aims of Moral Education among African Indigenous Societies

The African indigenous form of education had three main aims. These goals included equipping individuals with relevant knowledge and skills and proper codes of conduct that would enable them to be properly integrated in the society. Every step was taken to ensure that necessary skills, knowledge and especially proper codes of behaviour were learnt at specific stages as the individual progressed from childhood to adulthood and old age.

African indigenous education had a heavy component of moral education. The moral education was to orient individuals to community life, hence those moral values emphasized were communal in nature. Jomo Kenyatta (1953) stated that an individual who was self-centred was considered to be anti-social. Such a person was looked upon with suspicion and was not expected to prosper. Erny (1981) also noted in Chad that all, goods were destined for sharing and that no one was supposed to keep to himself more than he distributed to his family. Ocitti (1973) too observed that hospitality was priced among the Acholi people of Uganda. The Acholi people maintained that hospitality profited the one who gave more than the beneficiary.

African societies, by and large, also discouraged anti-social behaviours throughout the life of the individual. For instance, uncontrolled sexual behaviour was abhorred. African societies, therefore, censured uncontrolled sexual conduct. By and large, sexual relationships in most of the African traditional societies were confined to marriage. Sexual abuses such as adultery or fornication, incest and rape were viewed with such awe that people involved in these offences needed to be cleansed in a public ceremony. The public manner of handling such abuses and ridicule that followed, in some cases in form of ostracism of such individuals, minimised their occurrence.

Fidelity was one of the virtues treasured among African indigenous societies and especially that of the wife. Ocitti (1973) observed that among the Acholi people of Uganda, the qualities of a bride–to–be included fidelity and industriousness. Girls were trained to be honest and faithful to their husbands. In fact, women who could not control their sexuality risked staying unmarried.

The family institution in the traditional African societies was sacred and everything was done to ensure that it was intact. A family was not an individual affair. The whole society was concerned about stable family relationships. Traditional African societies believed that stable families were the corner-stones of a strong tribe or community. Children had to be born in a family and grow up in it. Therefore, having children out of wedlock was heavily censured.

Children were greatly treasured in African societies. Therefore, every effort was made to ensure that they were born and brought up in proper family set ups as children born out of wedlock were unaccepted. African traditional societies believed that a family was the best environment to nurture children and bring them up in acceptable moral conduct. In a family, the mother looked after the education of children during the first six years of life. Later, she concentrated on the education of girls while the father educated the sons.

Industriousness was greatly valued among indigenous African peoples of West Africa. For instance, from the myth of Eve on creation, we are informed that after God created man and woman, he gave them hoes and skills of hunting, farming and fishing so that they could work for their food. This would keep them away from stealing food. Stealing among Eve's people was punished severely by their God *'Manuga' (Brown et.al, 1975)*.

Among the Kikuyu, a man was not allowed to marry unless he had accumulated enough wealth as evidence that he would be able to cater for material needs of his family (Jomo Kenyatta, 1953). Although his parents were largely responsible for the bride price, he was supposed to chip in.

According to Ocitti (1973), the Acholi people of Uganda jeered at mothers who had lazy children and especially girls as follows:

> *The mother of this girl*
> *Dies on the way to the well*
> *On grinding stone*
> *In the fields picking firewood*
> *As if she has no children*
> *A hopeless daughter she has*
> *A daughter who has no manners*
> *Who is beautiful for nothing*
> *The mother of this girl*
> *Suffers all along*
> *As if she has not delivered*

Agents of Moral Education among the African Indigenous Peoples

Moral education of children started as soon as they were born. The mother impressed on the child the type of behaviour that was expected of him or her as he/she progressed from childhood to adulthood. Through lullabies and stories, the mother passed on to their young off springs cultural heritage of the family, clan, tribe and its heroic achievements. Graduation from one stage to another was based on age, knowledge and the intellectual maturity of the child. As the individual grew up graduating from one stage to another, they were expected to acquire and internalize the values that were prescribed by the society.

The father was an important agent of moral education and discipline. He was the symbol of authority. In many African societies, the father was the head of the family, and by virtue of this position in the family hierarchy coupled with his age, knowledge and experience, his authority was unquestioned. Indeed, children took their fathers more seriously than their mothers in matters of discipline. Mothers often reminded children that if they did not obey, she would report them to their father. The authority of the father was strengthened further by his religious position. Jomo Kenyatta (1953) stated that the father was the proper means of communication and fellowship with the ancestors. Man as the head of the family was regarded as the priest of the household and this entitled him to offer sacrifices. The consequences of offending the ancestral spirits resulted in misfortunes including death. Therefore, members of the family felt obliged to respect and obey the authority of the head of the family to avoid calamity befalling them and their families.

The institution of the family was very instrumental in the moral education of children. The family stood for values of the society and it ensured that their children adopted them. Acquisition of these values by a new generation guaranteed conformity with society's treasured beliefs and code of conduct. Children who deviated from what was expected or disobeyed their parents in anyway risked being cursed by them. Fear of being cursed enhanced obedience of children.

Rites of passage, which led to graduation of individuals from childhood to adulthood, were perhaps the most important medium of teaching and consolidating moral education. Until the child was ready to undergo puberty rites, education was primarily a family responsibility. During the rites of passage ceremony, the youth were removed from the society (and put in seclusion) so that all the important aspects of their tribal life could be impressed upon them without distraction. Education at this stage of life was highly formalized.

The content of education previously acquired by the individual through practical work, imitation, stories was now "confirmed", "completed" and in some way standardized into a coherent system. What was until now only an object of occasional teaching was "explained and communicated in a solemn manner". The trials of puberty rites taught the youth that they must carry pain, meet with misfortune and bear themselves like warriors.

After puberty rite of passage, these individuals were transformed into courageous young adults and were now expected to think and weigh all aspects of a situation before talking or acting. The spirit of comradeship was greatly strengthened due to the fact that they had undergone same pain together and shared similar knowledge and experiences. Therefore, each member of the age group regarded each other as a kin relative. They learnt to hunt, pick fruits, fish, cultivate, fetch firewood, socialise and dance together. This way, a high sense of cooperation and sharing was developed.

At this stage, the youth were provided with full information in matters of sex. This knowledge was necessary in preparing them for family life. They were properly instructed towards the choice of marriage partners. They were warned not to be misled by external beauty when looking for partners. Instead, they were advised to look for positive qualities in their prospective spouses, qualities such as honesty, industriousness, co-operation, courage, tolerance, and dependability. In particular, young men were reminded that it was their responsibility to take care of the family, parents, the weak and the elderly. They also got useful knowledge about medicinal herbs that could be administered to children and other people when they fell sick.

Reasons for the Success of Moral Education in Pre-colonial Africa

The success of moral education among African peoples was accomplished due to the fact that these societies had well defined goals on moral education. All socially sanctioned behaviour was known and was practised by everyone. There was no room for deviants. The methods of teaching were also very effective; they included lullabies, songs, proverbs, and stories. In fact, whatever was done or said had moral implications. Erny (1981) observed that members of African societies were compelled to lead morally accepted lives for fear of being psychologically and physically removed from society.

Fear of offending the ancestral spirits with unbecoming behaviour was also very effective in curtailing occurrence of prohibited behaviour. Showing disrespect to the ancestral spirits through misconduct left the individual open to wrath of the spirits (Erny, 1981). Everyone believed in the power of the spirits in punishing the wrong-doers.

Parents contributed a lot towards the success of moral education. They took up teaching very seriously. As earlier noted, the mother taught children during the first few years of life. Later, she continued with the education of girls while the father educated the boys. The parents knew the type of education society expected them to give their children and they transmitted it with modesty. Parents at the same time acted as models of good behaviour for their children.

Exemplary behaviour from parents and other grown-up members of the community contributed immensely in inducing good behaviour in the young members of the society.

Discipline was achieved through rewards, encouragement, counselling, and teaching via proverbs, maxims, riddles, stories and songs. Children learnt to be disciplined by internalising all the moral values contained in the songs, proverbs, riddles and other folklore unconsciously.

Finally, moral values of the African societies emanated from the society itself. Distant and rather abstract gods did not make laws for people to follow. People made laws. God only punished those who did not keep the laws made by people. People-made moral laws were for along time perceived to be humane and reasonable and therefore, people felt obliged to keep them.

Challenges of Teaching Moral Education in Modern Africa

The coming of Europeans to Africa led to the introduction of western type of education which failed to appreciate the moral teaching and rites of passage of the African people, particularly in the management of human sexuality and intimate relationships. The abandonment of traditional ways of life left a moral vacuum as the European way of life and formal education mainly concentrated on reading, writing and arithmetic and not on human values and relationships.

The introduction of formal education emphasizing reading, writing and arithmetic made many African parents feel incompetent to teach their children, for what they knew was no longer valued. The parents who insisted on their traditional ways of bringing up children found out that the school and the church tried to make children abandon what they had learnt from them. Unfortunately, even when more and more parents became "converted" to Christianity and adopted western ways of life, they did not feel confident and competent enough to teach the new western values because they had not grown in this kind of moral orientation. Thus, though Christian moral values are good, they have no socially inbuilt mechanisms to ensure that they are followed other than appeal to one's conscience.

Missionaries too did not collaborate with parents about the education of children. Parents, therefore, felt ignored and left the responsibility of moral education to churchmen and the school. Today, majority of parents have abdicated their role of teaching social and moral values, to teachers, churchmen and chance. Moral education in Africa today is in crisis; there are no clear-cut objectives as far as moral education is concerned and (laws) do not seem to apply to everyone equally. When there are no consistent methods of enforcing moral rules, moral teaching becomes very difficult if not impossible.

Another drawback to the teaching of moral education today is that moral values taught at the school system and churches are not rooted in the African cultural heritage. For instance, the Christian God makes rules for people and punishes them if they break the rules. The Christian God is very abstract and is not easily conceptualised. It is not surprising that some people swear using the bible that they are telling the truth while actually they are telling lies. In traditional societies, if you asked people to swear touching the soil that they are telling the truth, they would not if they knew they were telling lies. Even today many Africans will not swear touching the soil if they know they are cheating.

In traditional societies, people made rules and also punished those who broke them. Punishment and corrective measures were immediate. One did not wait for God to punish "for he may not punish soon enough for people to see". Often times, the Christian God does not seem to punish bad people for they appear to keep on living and thriving in wealth.

Today, the mass media have negatively influenced the society. In spite of their positive impact, some of the electronic media that is, television, movies and radio programmes portray negative behaviours. In addition, a substantial proportion of print media contain pornographic literature which is bad for children. Improved communication and transport systems by sea, land and air too, have allowed different people from different parts of the world holding different views on moral issues to come together and often interact. The result is divergent views regarding what kind of moral education to teach their young ones. This is unlike in traditional societies where people were in unison on moral issues. Today even individuals from one family may have different views on vital moral issues. These differences increase as one moves from one family to another and to society at large. For instance, one parent may try to teach her daughter to keep off from pre-marital sex, while another parent may introduce her daughter to birth control devices in order to avoid pregnancy. The two girls may be in the same school. The likely thing may be that the parent teaching her daughter to postpone sexual intimacy until marriage may lose out. Her daughter may not refrain from pre-marital sexual involvement because even the girl who indulges in pre-marital sex does not get pregnant because of birth control devices.

The role of men as fathers, head of families, figures of authority and protectors of moral values has been challenged. This is partly attributed to the concentration of most jobs in urban areas away from rural areas. Good proportion of men work in urban areas while their wives and children stay in rural homes. Men have, therefore, become `absentee' fathers and husbands. Consequently, men are not able to shape the behaviour of their children as they grow up. Lifestyle has also contributed to the weakening of the authority of men and older people on children. For example, even when men stay with their families in urban or rural areas, they spend most of their evening time, weekends, and public holidays in beer halls drinking, instead of being with their children. Because men are still looked upon as authority figures in the society, a good proportion of children do not take moral lessons and disciplines emanating from their mothers seriously.

Summary

The status of moral education among African societies depicts a state of crisis. There are no clear-cut goals on moral education. The teaching of moral education, that is, knowledge of what is right and wrong, one's obligations and rights to oneself and to others, including making responsible decisions, has almost been left to chance. Moral education, particularly in the area of intimate relationships, is wanting. Due to the neglect of teaching of moral education, African societies are experiencing social disorder and moral decay. Sexual crimes that were almost non-existent in traditional African societies such as rape, incest, homosexuality, prostitution are now very common This has led to the increase of sexually transmitted diseases (including AIDS, which has no cure), sexual violence resulting from jealousy and street children who are born out of casual sexual encounters.

Moral education was successful in African indigenous societies because it had clear cut goals and effective methods of teaching it. Therefore, it is important to harness progressive aspects of indigenous moral education into the mainstream of national education and national moral code. To do this, research into cultures and customs of ethnic groups in Black Africa should be carried out with a view to harnessing them into coherence for purposes of effectively teaching moral education.

In doing this, customs that have become controversial and outdated such as female circumcision should be substituted with a none-physical ceremony that would incorporate education about responsible human relationships especially intimate sexual relationships. This innovative initiative way of graduating girls into adulthood without circumcision is starting to take roots in Tharaka Nthi District in the Republic of Kenya (Waruru, 1999). Failure to manage and harness sexual energy into productive work and healthy relationships may in the near future wipe out the African race through sexually transmitted diseases particularly AIDS. By the year 2000, 30-40 million people worldwide were infected with HIV that causes AIDS and 70% of these were concentrated in sub-Saharan Africa (Republic of Kenya, 1997).

It should be noted that integration of progressive aspects of indigenous moral code into the educational system and religious moral code would provide the missing link in the promotion of sound moral education in modern Africa. Moral education, which is not rooted into people's way of lives or culture, has little or no chance of successfully and positively moulding people's morality. The role of culture in shaping people's lives should not be underestimated for it tells people in a given society who they are, where they have come from and where they want to go. People without a strong culture are therefore, like people wearing "borrowed clothes" and once the clothes are returned to their owners, they are left "naked" thereby leaving them exposed and vulnerable to all kinds of bad cultural influences.

However, it should be appreciated that moral education can only succeed if people and particularly parents and those in positions of power and leadership practise what they preach. In this respect, the whole society ought to rethink and outline sound moral values, which the older members must practise if they want the young to be bound by them.

Study questions

1. (a) Write a detailed account on how people of your community used to impart moral education on the incoming generation in pre-colonial Africa.

   (b) Evaluate the usefulness of strategies used by indigenous African society to teach moral education in contemporarily Kenyan society.

2. "Learning about moral education among African societies in pre-colonial Africa is a useless exercise". Evaluate the validity of this statement.

References

Brown, Godfrey N. and Hiskett (editors). (1975). *Conflict and Harmony in Tropical Africa*. London: George and Unwin Ltd.

Erny, Pierre. (1981). *The Child and His Environment in Black Africa*. Nairobi: Oxford University Press Ltd, 1981, Preface XVI

Kenyatta, Jomo. (1953). *Facing Mount Kenya*. Nairobi: Heineman Educational Books (East Africa Ltd).

Ocitti, P. J. (1973). *African Indigenous Education.* Nairobi: East African Literature Bureau.

Page, G. T., (1977). *International Dictionary of Education.* London: Nicholas Publishing Company.

Republic of Kenya. (1997). *Sessional Paper No.4 of 1997 on AIDS in Kenya.* Nairobi: Government Printer.

Waruru, Maina. (1999). "Alternative `Female Cut' Winning Acceptance," Nairobi: *Daily Nation*, Thursday 1st April.

7

Culture and Education

The Concept of Culture

The concept of Culture has been defined in different ways. Tylor (1902) defined culture as a complex whole which include knowledge, beliefs, art, moral, laws, customs and other capabilities acquired by man as man-made. This definition, while proclaiming culture as made by human beings, seemed to suggest that there is a universal culture. Boas (1940), however, argued that culture is specific to a particular society. He believed that each individual society has its own body of customs, beliefs and social institutions, instead of different societies having different degrees of universal culture. Good (1959) also defined culture as the aggregate of the social, ethical, intellectual, artistic, governmental and industrial attainments characteristic of a group or state or nation and by which it can be distinguished from or compared with others. Culture therefore, can be said to be the accepted way of living of a particular human group.

Some scholars, including anthropologists, have at times viewed culture as one entity common to all societies in the world. They argue that certain societies can be placed at the beginning of the continuum, others within the continuum and the rest at the extreme end, according to their degree of civilization. However, this view is not true. A more scientific view of culture shows that each individual society has its own body of customs, beliefs and institutions. Ezewu (1983:16) states that a person is born into a given society and learns the culture of that society.

Societies are unique, and so is their culture. Therefore, it is not fair to judge one society as weak or inferior just because the way of life of those particular people is different from ours. Instead, it is imperative that we strive to understand the internal dynamics operating in a given society. It is important to recognize that all societies have different cultures, and that a culture is distinguished by the society's special type of response to the problems which are common to all human beings. Thus, while a large variety of behaviour exists in every culture, the general or common form of behaviour such as honesty, respect, diligence and prudence will tend to vary from one society to another.

Culture is sometimes referred to as civilization. Mann (1983) associated civilization with the presence of some established social order as opposed to its absence. Thus, civilization connotes a state of human society characterised by a high level of intellectual, social, cultural development and civil order. In this case, a cultured man is synonymous with a civilized person. It is within this framework that the term culture is used to refer to advanced products of civilization such as literature, art and philosophy, and why educated people are described as cultured people. In this chapter, however, the concern is with culture as a composite of all that is passed down by human society from one generation to another in its material and the non-material perspectives.

The material culture is manifested in the objects used such as houses, dresses, sculpture, paintings, mode of transport, food and dietary habits among others. Non-mater culture, on the other hand, comprise facets like beliefs, customs and routines, value systems and mode of thinking, language, religion and other forms of expression.

Although these two aspects of culture, that is, the material and non-material are distinct and unique to individual cultures, today, there are certain elements that tend to be universal. For example, among the youth culture, there is the tendency to have a particular style of attire and grooming and speech mannerisms. In Kenya, for example, there is the evolution of the "sheng" language which is unique to youths both in the rural and urban set ups, and it cuts across the various socio-economic strata in society. This universality of certain elements of culture is made possible by modern technology, especially television.

Causes of Cultural Change

All cultures experience change. Nonetheless, modern societies experience more rapid cultural social change compared to traditional ones. Cultural change is brought about by both internal exogamous and external endogamous factors.

Endogamous change

Endogamous change is caused by factors that originate within a specific society. Some of the factors include technological innovation, ideology, cultural conflicts and planned change. These factors often bring with them significant changes in social organisations and social structure.

(a) Technological Innovations

Technologically induced culture is associated with inventions, which occur in technology, arts, music and the like. Examples of technology cultural products are computers, televisions, contraceptive pills, mobile telephones and so on. These technology based products have transformed people's way of life. For instance, television has made human interaction impersonal and in some cases very minimal for when people are watching television they are unlikely to talk to each other. People also have little time to visit others because television has become a "companion"

(b) Ideology

The term ideology often refers to a set of interrelated religious or political beliefs, values or norms that justify pursuit of a given goal. Ideologies have been used to direct change in a particular direction. For instance, conservative ideologies prefer maintenance of status quo. This outlook to life has a tendency to slow down social changes. Liberal ideologies on the other hand, seek for limited changes in social structure. For example, affirmative programmes seeking to redress gender imbalance in education, politics and employment are not aimed at major changes in the structure unlike the radical ideology that advocates total overall of all the social structures perceived to promote and perpetuate inequality.

Some individuals in the society have brought change using ideology. Leaders of countries such as the late Mao Tse Tung of China, Lenin in Soviet Union, and the current president of Cuba, Fidello Custro, have brought political as well as economical revolutions in their respective countries. Similarly, the late president of the Republic of Kenya, Jomo Kenyatta, used "harambee" philosophy (pulling/ working together) to harness resources from Kenyan communities in money, labour, and materials for socio-economic development. Through this ideology, many social facilities such as hospitals and schools were built between 1960's and 1970's.

(c) Social Cultural Conflicts

Conflicts within a society can also bring about change. Once a conflict is brought to the surface, ways and means of resolving it must be found. The solution agreed upon initiates the process of change. For example, Kenya teachers are likely to get salary increases from the government as a result of their fight for better terms of service.

(d) Planned Change

Education falls under planned change and is used to bring new ways of thinking about politics, work and general outlook to life through the curriculum in the school system. The school system is fairly effective in the achievement of this. For example, in many countries, educational system is often modified or completely changed to suit new situations. The education system in Kenya has undergone several changes since the attainment of political independence from Britain in 1963 in order to reflect the needs of the nation. An example, is the introduction of 8-4-4 system said to be more practical oriented (Ministry of Education, Science and Technology, 1984). The practical orientation of the curriculum was expected to equip its recipients with skills for self-employment because opportunities for salaried employment had reduced (Stabler, 1969). However, it has been noted that planned change through education is dependent on people's attitudes, material and human resources, and political dispensation among others. It has been observed that where planned change has occurred such as in China and Cuba, political will has been very critical.

Exogamous Cultural Change

Exogamous change refers to that is brought about by external factors. These external forces can be in form of biological and natural calamities and diffusion of ideas from more powerful cultures.

(a) Biological and Natural Calamities

Some of the natural catastrophes include: floods, droughts, landslides, and earthquakes, while biological disasters comprise emergence of new diseases like Ebola, AIDS and Severe Acute Respiratory Syndrome (SARS) among others.

The effects of natural and biological catastrophes depend upon their severity and ability of the society to absorb or react to them. These catastrophes are in themselves sudden and usually require people to make rapid readjustments in their behaviour. In case of AIDS people are expected to exercise restraint and practise use of safe sex methods such as condoms.

(b) Diffusion

Diffusion is the transmission of culture traits from one culture to another. It occurs wherever and whenever different cultures come into contact either in person or through mass media or exchange of items. It has been observed that direction of diffusion is rarely random or balanced among societies. On the whole, traits diffuse from more powerful to weaker people and from the more technologically advanced to less technologically advanced nations.

The foregoing discussion suggests that culture is dynamic. However, Ogburn (1962) noted that cultural change does not occur in any uniform manner. He observed that when culture begins to change, the modifications do not occur evenly in all the interrelated parts of cultural heritage. The unevenness in social change of different parts of culture is referred to as cultural lag.

According to cultural lag theory, change in material culture brought about by inventions, discoveries and technological developments by and large change culture faster than adaptive or non-material culture such as beliefs, laws, government and traditions. When different parts of culture, which are interrelated, experience change at varying rates, a strain is created between in unequally moving parts. The part that is moving at the slowest speed constitutes the cultural lag. Since the other parts of culture have already changed, the part that is lagging experiences adjustment. Analysis of social disorganisation in the contemporary society such as moral decay and failure of education to serve the needs of people can be attributed to irregular changes in the culture prompted by technological advancements.

Content of Culture

Some of the components of culture include speech, material traits, art, mythology and scientific knowledge, religious practices, family and social practices, property, government and warfare. An outline of each one of them is given hereunder.

(a) Speech

This includes languages and the writing system. Languages comprise not only verbal communication but gestures as well. Thus it is possible to distinguish between Arabic and Japanese systems of writing as well as their modes of speech.

(b) Material Traits

This component of culture includes food and dietary habits, dress and mode of grooming, utensils, weapons, types of shelter, television, vehicles and their style of construction among others.

(c) Art

Art is said to soothe the hearts of people because it expresses their feelings. In other words, art reveals the aesthetic value of a given society. Carvings, paintings, music and drawings comprise art.

(d) Mythology and Scientific Knowledge

Every society has its own myths and scientific discoveries. Some societies develop faster scientifically than others depending on the amount of scientific knowledge the society has.

(e) Religious Practices

These include modes of worship and view of the Creator, understanding of sickness, illness and the treatment of the sick, belief about death and the treatment of the dead.

(f) Family and Social Practices

Every society has its own methods of establishing relationships. Thus, customs and laws relating to marriage, inheritance of properties, regard for different sexes and their roles in society are found in human societies.

(g) Property

Property includes mode of production, standards of value, exchange and the different types of trade being practised.

(h) Government

This includes the national ideology and the political systems a society or nation practices. These change depending on the regime at any given time.

(i) Warfare

Societies had always been at war either due to external or internal tensions because of ideological differences, failure to share resources equitably and the like. This therefore, resulted in various types of weaponry and ammunitions being developed for the purpose of defence.

From the foregoing discussion, it is evident that the content of culture is quite extensive, diversified and permeates all aspects of life. At this point, therefore, it is important to discuss some of the outstanding characteristics of culture.

Characteristics of culture

1. Culture is a product of human interaction and therefore it is not inborn. The process of enculturation begins at birth. New members of the society become encultured through learning, living and by interacting with others, initially at family and extended family level and later with other institutions of the society such as the school, religious institutions, government and the like.

2. Culture extends beyond the life of each member of the society. Thus, the end of life span of an individual does not herald its "death". The living and newly enculturalized members continue to propagate their culture. Culture is therefore, said to be organic and supra-organic. It is a product of human interaction whose individual members have different life spans and therefore when some die, others continue to initiate new members into the cultural heritage.

3. Culture is cumulative and transmittable from one generation to the next by language and non-verbal symbols. This is possible due to human being's capacity to learn and to build upon the achievement of successive generations and thus guaranteeing cultured continuity.

4. Culture provides people with an identity. It tells them who they are, where they came from and where they are heading. It provides them with the power to create and recreate new ideas, values and products. In addition, culture equips people with knowledge and skills to help them satisfy their material, social, political and emotional needs.

5. Culture is both ideal and manifest. Ideal culture prescribes what people should do or conform to while manifest culture stands for actual behaviour of people. For instance, African societies prescribe marriage for people of marriageable age. However, the trend of remaining single is becoming increasingly common.

6. Culture is both adaptive and integrative. Culture must adapt for instance, to the environmental forces. Depending on people's

geographical region, they learn how to live in it. For example, those who live in cold places must dress up warmly to avoid perishing from it. Similarly, those who live in Kano plains in Nyanza province, Kenya, must find ways of dealing with floods during the rainy season. Culture also acts like adhesive in terms of common values. Commonality of certain values ensures that people view life from the same perspective. For instance, respect for human life is a universal value. Culture too must develop tolerance towards other people's views. This is particularly necessary in the modern world which is rapidly undergoing globalization and internationalization

7. Culture possesses some degree of stability and dynamism. Cultural aspects that contribute to stability include norms and value systems. Norms constitute guidelines for behaviour. For instance, people in a society are supposed to respect the rights of others and to maintain peace. These norms are passed from generation to generation to ensure continued harmonious co-existence. Values are aspects of culture perceived to be worthwhile in a given society. In Kenya, for instance, school education is valued as it is seen as a means for social mobility. Hardwork and "harambee" or pulling resources together for development, are some of the most important values in Kenya.

Education and Cultural Transmission

Education is a life-long process by which people learn new ways of thoughts and action. It encourages changes in behaviour which aim at improving the human condition. Education helps to instil self-confidence and self-reliance in an individual and allows for informed decision-making in such areas as health and nutrition, water and sanitation, and food production and its management. It is in this regard that education is recognized around the world as a basic pre-requisite for development (GOK/UNICEF; 1992:95).

Education can be looked at from the formal, non-formal and informal aspects. The formal aspect is represented by institutions like schools, colleges and universities which inculcate knowledge, skills and attitudes into the young ones that are acceptable in the society.

This is achieved through the content of the school curriculum. The non-formal education refers to activities usually found outside traditional schooling in which content is adapted to unique needs of the students or unique situations such as women's groups. The activities involved in this kind of a setting are not only educational but also assist in generating income. Some activities are also for recreational purpose, for example, singing and dancing (Sifuna, 1980).

The informal facet of education is the type of learning that one finds among peer groups. In traditional societies, this was the mode of educating the young into the societal accepted norms. In a school environment, for instance, this kind of education goes on in social clubs, sports and games. Outside the school system, the "Jua Kali" sector is an informal system of education. Apprentices in motor mechanics and other activities are also included in this sector (King, 1974).

Education can be said to belong to the process of enculturation, whereby the young ones are initiated into the culture of their given society. In this discussion, however, we shall limit ourselves to the formal aspects of education generally referred to as schooling.

Schools are set up by a society to selectively transmit those values and knowledge that a society determines as appropriate. This is done through the programmes contained in the curriculum. The curriculum, therefore, can be viewed as a planned document through which the values of a given society are transmitted in a school setting. It is through the school that a society provides specialized training for its young members. Thus education is concerned with the total training of the whole personality of an individual, that is, the physical, mental, emotional and spiritual characteristics of a person.

Education has several functions. Some of these strive to enhance creativity and critical thinking, develop personality of an individual, improve the general living of not only an individual but also the nation, and conserve and transmit aspects of cultural heritage that is valued. It is this conserving function of education that is discussed here. Education has the task of transmitting cultural values and behaviour patterns of a society to its young members. It is through this process that a society achieves some form of basic social conformity and at the same time ensures that its modes of life are preserved. This is what is usually referred to as the conservative function of education. It is conservative in the sense that it is only concerned with transmitting from one generation to the next, the values that exist without fundamental changes.

As earlier mentioned, education encourages and promotes creativity. Youths are encouraged to develop critical thinking. This is because a society needs critical and creative thinkers who can make inventions, discoveries and initiate positive change. Universities, for example, are not just institutions where knowledge is transmitted but also institutions where knowledge is created and discussed for proper and useful implementation. Thus, education does not only respond to social changes but is a factor that brings about social change.

Education has also the function of minimizing cultural lag. As we saw earlier, Cultural lag refers to the tendency of some areas of culture to change more slowly than others. For instance, different communities within a nation do not adopt new ideas at the same pace. In a multi-ethnic nation such as Kenya, it has been observed that some communities have embraced school education while others have not. Consequently, individuals and communities are at different levels of cultural transformation. The Maasai, for example, a pastoralist community in Kenya, seem to accept change at a slower pace than other communities such as the Agikuyu, the Luo, the Kamba and Kisii. This state of affairs makes a nation less integrated thereby creating strains in the society. The role of education is, therefore, to ensure that people within a nation have more or less same knowledge, skills, beliefs and value systems.

To achieve meaningful cultural integration, all efforts should be made to ensure that education is made available to all citizens. This is important because individuals who have not gone through an education system are less prepared for coping with technological changes. Therefore, socially deprived people, the poor and women generally should be helped to acquire education through bursaries and other special programmes. Special programmes include school feeding programmes, provision of milk for children, building of mobile schools in areas occupied by nomadic peoples, construction and financing of boarding schools for primary and secondary students in sparsely occupied areas of the country such as North Eastern Kenya and building of single-sexed schools for girls and boys. Some communities, especially, the Muslims, do not allow most of their girls after the age of puberty to attend co-educational schools for fear of pregnancy and sexual harassment by male colleagues. Even the more liberal communities fear that their daughters will be sexually molested by their male counterparts in co-educational schools. Such cases have been reported in Kenya (Mackenzie, 1991).

Education must mould people to become problem-solving oriented rather than consumers of knowledge. People educated using problem solving approaches such as project work, demonstrations, research work and discussions are more prepared to learn all the time and cope with social change. Education therefore, does not end with schooling; it is a life-long process.

Culture and the School Curriculum

Culture forms the content of socialization and education. In the case of the school, culture is the curriculum. Sociologists, therefore, have made the following observations about culture and the school curriculum, that is, subjects taught in schools and the cultural values they transmit.

(a) Languages

Communication is more than just talking. Whatever is being said must be understood. Hence, communication is the transmitting of thoughts, ideas and feelings from one mind to another. Communication has been referred to as the lifeblood of a society. Society, therefore, must provide its members with the tools of communication. Thus, the teaching of language(s) in schools is crucial for socialization and education. In Kenyan schools, English and Kiswahili are compulsory.

(b) Agricultural Sciences, Vocational and Technological Courses

Members of a society must feed themselves and improve their conditions of living by working on their environment–Hence, the necessity for the teaching of such disciplines as agriculture sciences, vocational and technological courses. In Kenyan primary schools, a lot of emphasis is put on these subjects–Kenya being predominantly an agricultural country.

(c) Aesthetic Values

Every society has its own ways of promoting and appreciating beauty. Aesthetic values are unique to each individual societies. Music, sculpture among others vary from one society to another. Schools promote and assist students to appreciate aesthetic values by teaching of subjects such as arts and music. These subjects also assist students to learn meaning of communicating feelings.

(d) Religious Education

The desire to worship is inherent in all human beings. Hence society must provide religious education to meet the spiritual needs of its members. Social education and ethics is also taught in Kenyan schools to supplement religious education. The purpose of this subject is to assist students appreciate moral values other than religious teaching. The argument for this subject is that people can be religious but not necessarily moral.

(e) Geography and Natural Sciences

The physical environment is, in reality, the main source of livelihood for any given society. For people to fully benefit from it, they must master it properly. This, therefore necessitates the teaching of Geography and the Natural sciences to pupils and students. This enables them to be masters of their own environment early enough and thus act on it accordingly.

(f) Social Sciences

Subjects such as history, sociology, anthropology and other social sciences impact knowledge that enables members of any given society to co-exist under acceptable social conditions. These subjects, therefore, help to prepare young people for better living.

(g) Building and Surveying Courses

Shelter is one of the basic needs for all human beings. Every society has its own form and design of shelter. The teaching of these courses assists members of the society to construct good shelters suitable to their physical environment and geographical climate.

(h) Governance and Social Control

Governance and rulership are features found in all societies. No society can survive without rule and order. Every society must therefore regulate itself in order to ensure its continued existence. The school system does this through the teaching of good governance and the study of the procedures of social control such as law.

From the foregoing discussion, it is very clear that schools have a formidable task of transmitting acceptable societal cultural values. Society places a lot of expectations on the schools, some of which cannot be accomplished by the schools. This is made difficult particularly by the social stratification phenomenon which categorizes schools into different socio economic levels. Thus, the transmission of the same type of values on the same wave length becomes somehow difficult. Furthermore, this process of cultural transmission by schools is made complex by competition with other transmission agencies such as peer groups, religious organizations and the mass media. Some of these agencies, especially the mass media, can command a more powerful influence on the pupils than schools.

Summary

Culture clearly is the sum total of a people's way of life at a given time. An individual learns the Culture of the society through the process of socialization, thereby adopting the society's unique way of life. Education on the other hand, includes every process that helps to form a person's mind, character and physical development. Education can be either formal or informal and in non-formal way. The informal aspects include the socialization processes that occur outside the school system such as games and social clubs. The formal aspects are the ones we refer to as schooling (are in form of school subjects such as, mathematics, agriculture, biology, Kiswahili among others).

A school is a social institution which is bureaucratically arranged by society to selectively transmit those values and knowledge that the society considers appropriate. The curriculum is the content of those social values. In addition, schools also have a responsibility to develop creative and critical thinking.

Society, culture and education are interrelated and each is necessary for the continued existence of the others. Society has the responsibility of producing and teaching its members vital aspects of culture in terms of knowledge, skills and value systems for holding the society together. To do this, society expresses its culture and teaches it to the members. In this way, transmitting culture becomes education itself, as education is not possible without a living culture and society.

Study questions

1. Define the concept of culture.
2. Using relevant examples, examine the relationship between education and culture.

References

Ezewu, E. (1986). *Sociology of Education.* London: Longman.

GOK/UNICEF, (1992). *Children and Women in Kenya: A Situational Analysis.* Nairobi: Regal Press Limited.

King, K. (1974). "Skill Acquisition in the Informal Sector of the Economy", in Court and Dharam, *Education, Society and Development: New Perspectives from Kenya.* Nairobi: Oxford University Press.

Ogburu, W., and Nimkaff, M.F. (1960). *A Handbook of Sociology.* New York: Routledge.

Mann, Micheal. (1983). *Macmillian Student Encyclopedia of Sociology.* London' Macmillan Press.

Sheffer, Norman. (1975). *Many Cultures, Many Heritages.* Montreal: MCGraw-Hill Ryerson Limited

Ministry of Education, Science and Technology. (1984). *8-4-4 System of Education.* Nairobi: Government Printer.

Sifuna, N. D. (1986). *Education in Kenya: A brief Survey.* Nairobi: A paper presented at the second workshop on co-operation for Education and Training in Eastern and Southern Africa.

Stabler, E. (1969). *Education since Uhuru* Midletow Connecticut, Wesleyan university press

Tylor E.B. (1902) *Primitive Culture.* 4th Edition John Murry

8

Education and Social Stratification

Definition of Social Stratification

Social stratification refers to the division of members of society into social layers of ranks or strata. An ascribed status is one occupied by an individual by right of birth, while an achieved status is one occupied by a person as a result of his/her personal efforts in society. A good number of African societies combine both. However, achieved status is increasingly becoming more dominant over ascribed status for it is based on school education. By and large, those who attain higher levels of education have better chances of social mobility as well as occupational mobility.

Depending on the particular society, individuals can move either from one stratum to another or within the same stratum. Such movements or change of status is called social mobility but where individuals move within a stratum, such movement is called horizontal mobility. Social movement from a low to high social class status is called vertical mobility while high to low status is referred to as downward mobility. There are four main types of social stratification: slavery, caste, estate, and social class.

Slavery

Slavery is a legalized form of social in-equality for individuals or groups. Enslaved people are legally owned by others and their status is transferred from parents to children.

People in-servitude are treated just as if they are household pets or household items. Main sources of slaves in the past were the captives of war and piracy. In the contemporary world, individuals who cannot withdraw their labour are said to be in bonded slavery. Bonded labourers are imprisoned in employment as they struggle often throughout their lifetime to repay debts.

Other categories of people perceived to be in servitude include labourers and maids working in foreign countries. Their employers often hold their passports and subject them to unpleasant working conditions and threaten them with deportation if they decide to quit. Illegal immigrants in the industrialized countries are also under constant threat of deportation if they protest about poor working conditions. In the recent past, young women from Eastern Europe and Africa have been lured to Europe for employment only to find themselves trapped into organised prostitution. It is estimated that at least 2.7 million people were still enslaved at the beginning of the 21st century (Schaefer, 2003).

Caste

This is a social class system which exists in traditional India and it is the most rigid form of social stratification. For instance, mobility from one level in society to another is extremely difficult, if not impossible. Individuals are born into a position in the hierarchy and roles are ascribed without regard for that person's unique characteristics or talents. The caste system is justified on religious grounds.

Estate or Feudal System of Stratification

This type of stratification is based on land tenure. Land is held by the landlords. The poor and the landless are allowed to use the land in return for free domestic and military services. The landless, and especially in less industrialised countries, are usually at the bottom of the social hierarchy.

Social Class and Stratification

This is the system of dividing people into social ranks on the basis of level of education, occupation and income. Using income, level of education and occupation, people in modern societies have been put in three major categories namely, those in high socio-economic status comprising the rich and the very rich; middle socio-economic status encompassing moderately rich; and the low socio-economic status group, that is, the poor and those with low or little education. In all the three categories, education solidifies the class standing of an individual. Generally, education is a means of achieving high social status. It is important to note that social classes normally used by Kenyan advertisers and members of society at large have been "borrowed" from those of United Kingdom although the Kenyan social classes have not yet solidified as much as those of United Kingdom. According to Rogers (1987), six social grade classification exist in United Kingdom. These include:

A. *Upper Middle Class:* This comprises heads of households who are usually successful business people, professional senior civil servants, airline pilots, and university professors. This category of people may even have a substantial private income. They live in suburban areas in large detached houses or in towns in expensive flats or houses. This class constitutes about 3% of the population.

B. *Middle Class:* These are senior people and are almost at the top of their chosen business professions. They form about 13% of the population, are usually well paid and are regarded as `well off, with a life-style that is generally respectable rather than luxurious.

CI. *Lower Middle Class:* People in this class include small traders, non-manual workers, and white-collar job workers constituting about 22%. Those in this category are mainly supervisors, administrators, clerical staff and often middle management people.

C2. *Skilled Working Class:* These are manual workers who possess skills that are normally acquired after serving an apprenticeship. They are also referred to as blue collar workers and they constitute about 31% of the population

D. *Semi-skilled and Unskilled Working Class:* All manual workers who are generally unskilled, or those needing minimum of skills to carry out their daily jobs belong to this class. They constitute 19% of the population

E. *Lowest Subsistence level category:* These are old age pensioners who only have a state pension, widows and their families, casual workers, and unemployed. These form 11%, and are dependent on social security and other state schemes, or have very small private means for their upkeep.

Using United Kingdom's social categories, the following social grade classifications have emerged in Kenya. These are:

AB= These are the fully qualified professionals, senior managers, senior government officers, university lecturers, owners of large businesses and graduate secondary school teachers.

C1= This category includes middle/junior managers, foremen, qualified technicians, nurses, owners/ managers of medium sized firms and untrained graduate teachers of Bachelor of Arts/Bachelor of Science calibre.

C2= This group comprise skilled manual workers, mechanics, carpenters, non-graduate teachers, that is, P_1 and P_2, with basic four (4) years and two (2) years of secondary school education respectively junior clerks, chiefs and owners of small firms.

D= This classification is made up of semi-skilled manual workers, house servants, waiters, shop-assistants, and forestry workers.

E= This class of people is occupied by subsistence farmers, unskilled workers, casual labourers, and the landless.

McCann-Erickson (1997), used these social classes to study the needs and motivations of the Kenyan youth for the purpose of establishing their present and future consumer behaviour. Sociologists and sociology of education scholars should try and validate these social classes in order to establish how they impact on the academic performance of children.

Definitions of Social Class

Different scholars have come up with different definitions of a social class. Max Weber defined a class as an aggregate of people who have similar life chances or opportunities to education, jobs and positions of power. He identified three elements of social stratification namely: class, status, and power. People belong to a class when they share economic interests in the society.

Status, which is a second element of social stratification, concerns itself with the respect, social honour and deference given to individuals and groups. Sometimes, status is achieved and is linked to occupations. University professors, for example, usually have a high status in Kenya even though they do not earn a lot of income like bank managers and politicians. Their high status seems to come from their expert knowledge rather than economic power.

Other kinds of status are ascribed and beyond the control of the individual. In African traditional societies, for instance, old people had a higher status than the young. Generally, males tend to enjoy a higher status than females.

Political power is a third element of social stratification. This refers to the ability to make decisions which will affect other people. This kind of power is often exercised by governments and heads of various organizations in the society. Its most obvious application is in central and local government, though it may also exist in other forms and places. A head teacher, for example, generally has political power both inside and outside school. He/she can take decisions involving the future of teachers, pupils and by implication their families. He/she often plays a separate political role in the community.

Karl Marx, on the other hand, defines a social class as an aggregate of people who stand in the same relationship to the means of production such as, land, factories, mines among others. The most important criterion for determining such relationship is the issue of the ownership and control of the means of production.

In the feudal societies the landlords dominated the landless. In the industrial societies, the *bourgeoisies* (the owners of means of production and employers of wage-labour) dominate the *proletariat* or the wage earners. According to Karl Marx, there is always class struggle between the "haves" and "have nots". Max Weber, unlike Karl Max, argued that social relations during any period in history were mainly shaped by the individuals who controlled primary mode of production such as land or factories. He also argued that class relations and exploitation of workers could be eliminated if workers did away with "false consciousness" an attitude held by members of a class that does not accurately reflect their predicament. According to Karl Marx, this should be replaced by *"class consciousness"*–a subjective awareness held by members of a class regarding their common vested interests and need for collective political action to bring about social change.

Social Class and Equality of Educational Opportunity

Equality of educational opportunity is not something that starts suddenly when compulsory education begins. Equalities in opportunity for educational development may arise out of any of these particular factors, namely, familial, economic, class, regional and sex. The chances of being born and of staying alive are relatively greater the higher up the social scale one goes. There is evidence that infant care and use of medical services improve considerably as one passes from the lower manual working-class mother to the upper middle-class mother. Thus, if the child's total biological constitution is undermined either out of ignorance or carelessness or lack of proper medical care then the child's general health may be compromised thus hampering his/her educational progress.

Parental interests and aspirations for their child's education are important. The children who are encouraged in their work by their parents seem to be at an advantage both in the relatively high scores they make in their tests and in the way they improve their scores between eight and eleven years compared to those who are not encouraged (Morrison and Mclutyre, 1971:37). This interest is related to the parents' social-economic and cultural status and to a large extent, educational levels.

Language and social class cannot be separated. Linguistic inadequacy is closely associated with the home and social background. This in turn affects the eliciting of intellectual potential. Basil Bernstein (1961), noted that children from the working class have a different language compared to those from the middle and upper classes. The working class children tend to use a restricted code whose characteristics include: short sentences; simple and repetitive conjunctions such as, "and", "so," "then", "because," as well as repeated use of short comments and questions. Again, they are not able to express themselves abstractly, and they make statements that are broken up with such stabilizers such as "you see", "you know", in order to gain confidence. On the other hand, middle class children use quite an elaborate code which is shown by complex sentences with many adjectives, adverbs, and adjectival and adverbial clauses. They are also able to sustain a conversation for a long time, express themselves abstractly, and manifest logical trend of thoughts.

The Influence of Social Class on School Academic Performance

Emile Durkheim (1956) maintained that there were as many different kinds of education as there are social classes in any given society. Social class in modern societies is determined by such factors as the level of education, occupation and income. Individual families are differentiated by educational level, occupation, as well as the income level of the family.

The social class of an individual will affect the individual's attitudes and values in life, including school education. It has been established that people of high socio-economic status send their children to school earlier than those of low socio-economic status. This is attributed to the fact that they have the resources to spend on nursery education for age three children. Poor parents on the other hand, send their children later or not at all. The majority of parents in the rural areas do not send their children to nursery schools at all. A study conducted in Kenya by Gakuru (1977), revealed that wealthier and better-educated parents send their children to private nursery schools and create a conducive learning environment at home. This puts their children at an advantage in school work compared to children of poor parents. Generally, children from families of high socio-economic status are often more ready to learn and consequently stand a better chance of succeeding in their studies.

The high socio-economic class have the financial ability to provide their children with books and other related educational materials. These children are widely exposed to other educational information, for example, from the radio, television, videos and computers. In addition, they attend good public schools with highly qualified teachers and good facilities. Examples of these national schools in Kenya are Mangu High School, Alliance Boys, Loreto Limuru and Kenya High School. Children with parents in high social economic statuses often attend such schools. The children who attend these schools do so because they have had good educational background in nursery and primary schools. Somerset (1974), shows that a large number of those who go to these secondary schools are ones with well educated parents.

Most children from higher socio-economic class do well in their examinations. Even if they do not pass well, such children still end up in these good schools because their parents have the socio-economic influence. Cost-sharing introduced in Kenya in 1988 whereby parents were expected to contribute substantially to the provision of education in terms of buying books and provision of educational facilities, was making it impossible for children from poor socio-economic status to attend good schools because of the high fees required.

Well equipped and staffed secondary schools provide good chances of qualifying for tertiary level education especially university, thus guaranteeing access to higher education and consequently access to prestigious occupations and high income. In this way, children from high socio-economic status families are likely to retain that status themselves and pass it on to their own offspring. Other factors and their effects on educational performance as well as on social stratification are described below.

Encouragement in School Education

Children who are not encouraged by parents in their school work are likely to go to school late, for they may be given duties to perform before going to school. Such duties include fetching water, opening the family shop, cooking and even bathing younger sisters and brothers. Sometimes such children go to school late because of being burdened with a lot of household chores. Constant late-attendance of school is bound to have an adverse effect on academic achievement.

On the other hand, children from high socio-economic status are prepared for school early, are well fed and driven to school in a car. Their parents show a lot of concern to poor academic performance. Thus, the parents take time to help their children with their homework and inspire them to achieve high educational goals.

Provision of a Good Model of English

The language spoken at the homes of the parents from high socio-economic class is often the medium of instruction in schools therefore; children from this class have an advantage over children who speak mother tongue at home. Apart from the language of instruction in schools being the same as the language spoken at home, parents from the high socio-economic status are able to buy their children books which parents from low-socio-economic class cannot afford. These further increase their children's chances to acquire more language for educational purposes.

School Activities

Good schools in terms of availability of human and physical materials, always have many co-curricular activities that offer opportunities for students to acquire more knowledge. Poorly equipped schools do not have many co-curricular activities. Parents from high socio-economic status quite often finance school programmes such as construction of swimming pools, field trips including exchange education programmes for their children.

Academic and Job Aspirations

Many research findings have indicated that the academic aspirations of the school child are positively related to the socio-economic status of his/her parents. This is because educational provision is closely linked with class, power and status of its recipients. High and middle class parents do not discriminate sending girls to school. Girls in these families are sent to good schools just as boys. In fact, such girls are not expected to marry early. They are not even overburdened with household chores since their parents can afford to engage the services of household helps.

Education and Social Stratification: Colonial Africa

In colonial Africa, those who received western kind of education eventually had advantage over those who did not receive it. The majority of those who received this education were the Christians converts. In Kenya, those who benefited were dwellers in some coastal areas and those in places with good, cool climate in Eastern, Rift Valley, Central and Western parts of the country. Chiefs who accepted Western type of education had their people socially advantaged. Kikuyu chiefs accepted Western education more readily than the Maasai.

Education and Social Stratification in Post-Colonial Era

In many countries, universal education is not practised. This favours certain groups while others are disadvantaged. The educated population are able to compete well in the modern labour market at the expense of those who were unable to attend school. This situation brings about differences of income between those who are employed and those who work in subsistence agriculture or in the informal urban sector, resulting in emergence of social strata. Thus, a clear distinction exists between the schooled and the non-schooled. Even where basic education is universally practised, differences still exist at post-primary levels.

There is no African country that has achieved universal secondary education. In addition, the recruiting and gate-keeping mechanisms, for instance, national examinations, still stifle the transition from primary to the secondary education. However, even if universal secondary education is practised, the same watershed of transition between secondary education and university is still intact. It is therefore not possible to give equal level of education standards to every member of the society. Quantitative differences between education are reinforced by the tendency of children to drop out at each level of education. Drop-out rates tend to be particularly high among poorer members of the society and especially, those in the rural areas. The major reason for drop-out rates being relatively high among lower income groups is that pupils cannot afford to remain in schools.

Even when parents do not pay school fees for their children, there are usually uniform costs, transport and food costs. Thus, children from poorer families are often not able to attend free schools because they need to be working to support themselves and their families. Girls are particularly disadvantaged because they are often required to do domestic duties and parents are often afraid that the longer they stay in school, the higher their chances of getting pregnant. For example, among, the Pokot, being illiterate especially among the girls/women a few years ago was seen as fashionable. Education was equated with disobedience (*Daily Nation,* 23/8/95). Unfortunately, the situation has not changed much. Most communities prefer to invest in the education of boys than that of girls. The incentives to be in school for longer periods for girls are less than those of boys because they are less perceived as likely to get good employment.

Besides girls being disadvantaged, rural schools suffer a number of educational inequalities. In the first place, visitations from school inspectors or quality standards officers are not regular. Secondly, children in rural areas do not have complementary learning experiences such as school debates on television, unlike their colleagues in urban areas. Thirdly, repeating of classes among students of lower social economic groups in rural areas, and particularly the females, is quite common. Most children from the upper and middle classes proceed to the next level of education much faster than their rural colleagues.

Pre-primary Education

Pre-primary education promotes differences in quantity and quality of education. Nursery schools, which are usually attended for two or three years before a child joins primary school, tend to be patronized mainly by children from high socio-economic strata because they can afford the exorbitant fees charged by proprietors of these institutions. The Kenyan government does not provide for pre-primary education. Thus, the parents who are able to provide this education give their children a head start that permits them to gain entry to good primary schools.

Private Schools

These schools maintain and increase social stratification. Private schools have a wide varying range in quality and fees structures, and have different sponsors. They produce excellent results due to the good facilities available, well qualified teachers and high level of discipline among students. Private schools are categorized into: the private high-cost and the private low-cost. Most of the private low-cost schools are commercially operated with poorly trained teachers and inadequate facilities. They are often established in or near downtown noisy environment which is not conducive for learning. The criterion for attending private schools depends on the parents' ability to pay fees.

Boarding Schools

Pupils or students in boarding schools remain within the environment of a school for longer period, than the day scholars and therefore they tend to have a greater impact on their attitudes. Since the schools usually give high quality education with good examination results, they also facilitate entry of their students into good university programmes such as medicine, law, engineering among others. These fields of study often lead the beneficiaries to be deployed in powerful administrative positions in government and private sectors.

Mixed Secondary Schools

Research has shown that girls in mixed schools, especially those that are not high cost tend, to perform poorly as compared to their male counterparts. Due to their upbringing, girls are culturally supposed to be shy and not vocal. In class, they keep off participating in discussions. Besides academic problems, they are taken advantage of by their male colleagues and male teachers. A good example of this was the sexual harassment that girls were subjected to by their male colleagues at St. Kizito secondary school, in Meru in Eastern Province, Kenya in 1991 (Mackenzie, 1993:35). During this incident, 19 girls died due to suffocation in the crush while 71 were raped.

The Vocational Education Fallacy

Although vocational education is said to be a panacea to unemployment, it often adds to social stratification. It has been observed that those with less academic abilities end up in vocational training institutions, while those with academic abilities follow the academic route, that is, join secondary school and eventually the university.

Vocational education is more expensive due to the practical materials needed, coordination and implementation. This type of education also promotes social stratification in that; those students who are academically and financially poor are the major recipients. The graduates of vocational education in salaried employment earn less compared to their counterparts who follow academic education.

Summary

It is quite evident from the foregoing discussion that educational provision is closely linked with the recipients' class, power and status. Governments that wish to reduce these social disparities need strategies and policy measures both within the education system and outside it. Within the system, specific efforts can be made to promote education of poorer groups by offering scholarships. Education in rural areas and education of females can be encouraged by specific programmes such as building of single sexed schools for girls. Thirdly, efforts must be made to reduce the discriminatory aspects of education and to spread quality as uniformly as possible. Outside the education system, health programmes and school feeding programmes should be enhanced and promoted. These will assist in improving the prosperity of poorer groups and minimize some stratifying factors such as school dropouts. Also, efforts to reduce disparities in incomes can play an important role in reducing social stratification, and thus facilitate equal opportunities in education achievement. It must, however, be noted that as much as those measures are noble and even attainable to some extent, they would encounter opposition from the existing elite.

Education as discussed above enhances stratification in society by allocating jobs to those with higher educational qualifications. Education is thus seen as a factor that enhances and promotes change while at the same time making sure that the status quo is maintained.

Study questions

1. Define the concept of "social stratification" and discuss its implication on allocation of educational resources.
2. Examine the relationship between parental socio-economic status and academic educational opportunities for their children.
3. Elaborate the effect of language on equality of educational opportunity.

References

Becker, H. S. (1952). "Social Class Variations in Pupil Variations in Pupil-Teacher Relationships", *Journal of Educational Sociology*, Vol. xxv.

Bernstein, B. (1971). *Class, Codes and Control*. London: Routledge and Kegan Paul.

Brophy, J.E. and Good, T. L. (1974). *Teacher-Student Relationships*. New York: Holt, Rinehart and Winston.

Burstall, C. (1968). *French from Eight: A National Experiment*, Slough: N.F.E.R.

Bush, R. N. (1954). *The Teacher-Pupil Relationship*. New York. Printice Hall.

Dahrendorf, R. (1964). Recent Changes in class structure of European societies, *Daedalus* Vol. 93. No.1, Winter, pp.225-70.

Davison, H. and Land, G. (1960-61). Children's Perceptions of their Teachers, *Journal of Experimental Education*.

Dore, R. (1975). *The Diploma Disease, Education Qualification and Development*. Berkeley: University of California Press.

Durkheim, E. (1956). *Education and Sociology*. Glencoe: Free Press.

Farrant, S. J. (1964). *Principles and Practice of Education.* London: Longman Group.
Flanders, N. A. (1970). *Analysing Teacher Behaviour.* New York: Addison Wesley.
Freire, Paulo. (1972). *Pedagogy of the Oppressed.* London: Penguin Books.
Goodacre, E. J. (1968). *Teachers and their Pupils' Home Background.* Slough, N.F.E.R.
Gakuru, O.N. (1977). *Pre-Primary Educational and Access to Educational Opportunities in Nairobi.* Nairobi: University of Nairobi, Institute of Development Studies, College of Humanities and Social Sciences.
Grieger, R. M. (1971). Pygmalion Revisted: A Loud Call for Caution, *Interchange*, Vol. II
Grindal, B. T. (1972). *Growing up in Two Worlds: Education and Transition among Sisala of Northern Ghana.* New York: Holt, Rinehart and Winston.
Kaplan, L. (1952). The Annoyances of Elementary School Teachers, *American Journal of Sociology,* Vol. XI.
Keddie, N. (1972). "Classroom Knowledge" in Young M.F.D (Ed) *Knowledge and Control: New Directions for Sociology of Education.* London: Collier Macmillan.
Manase, T. J. and Kisanga, E. S. (1978). An Insight into Disciplinary Problems in Schools in Tanzania in *Papers in Education and Development, No.5.* University of Dar es Salaam, Department of Education, August.
McCann-Erickson. (1997). *The McCann-Erickson Youth Hotline: keeping you in touch with Kenya`s youth.* Nairobi; McCann-Erickson.
Omondi, N. Lucia. (1999). *Language and Life: A Linguistic Glance at Kenya, Inaugural Lecture,* Presented at University of Nairobi on 30th September 1999 in the Multi- purpose (8-4-4) Lecture Theatre.
Rogers, len. (1987). *Handbook of Sales and Marketing management. London:* Kogan Page Ltd.
Sadker, M. P. and Sadker D. M. (Ed) (1982). *Sex Equity Handbook for Schools.* New York: Longman, Inc.

Scotter, Richard, D. Van, et.al. (1991). *Social Foundations of Education*. Boston: Allyn and Bacon.

Waller, Willard. (1932). *The Sociology of Teaching*. New York: John Wiley and Sons, Inc.

White, R. K. and Lippit R. (1960). *Autocracy and Democracy: An Experimental Inquiry*. New York: Harper.

9

The Sociology of the Classroom

The Characteristics of the Classroom

The classroom means a room in which a group of pupils who are more or less in the same position, in terms of age or class within a school, system are taught. The school on the other hand, stands for the physical facilities, teachers, pupils and supportive staff in the institution of learning. Both physical and human resources in the school make pedagogy possible. A school can therefore be defined as a social institution set aside by the society for the purposes of providing education.

A classroom is a subset of the school and has teachers and pupils who operate in relation to each other. The teacher is the key figure in the classroom. The main role of the teacher is to instruct and assess pupils who may have come from different socio-economic status and with diverse intellectual endowments in cognitive skills in terms of facts and skills. Besides teacher's pedagogical role, she/he represents the adult world of authority and is expected to acquaint pupils with proper codes of behaviour in the classroom, school, and the society.

Patterns of Teacher-Pupil Interactions

Teacher-pupil interactions have been studied from the leadership perspective provided by the teacher, pedagogical methods employed by the teacher and interaction dynamics between the teacher and children of different socio-economic status (SES). We begin our discussion with teacher-pupil interactions from leadership style perspective.

Leadership can be defined as an ability of a person to guide and also exert authority on other people. Authority here refers to the right to command and enforce obedience. It is fair to say that, without some form of leadership, a large amount of human activity, including learning, is directionless and confused. In creating order and direction in the classroom, a teacher can utilize a number of leadership styles, that is, democratic, authoritarian and laissez faire. Each of these leadership styles offers different learning experiences as well as outcomes. Kurt Lewin Lippit, and White in 1939 developed the study of leadership styles namely: democratic, authoritarian, and laissez-faire and their effects on people'sbehaviour. The study utilized experimental groups of eleven year old boys, who met for six weeks under a leader who employed either democratic, autocratic or a laissez-faire leadership style. Each group was exposed to each of these leadership styles in turn with the same leaders adopting different styles. Detailed records of the behaviour of the boys in the groups was kept. The findings revealed that different styles of leadership produced different groups and individual behaviours.

Democratic Leadership Style and its Influence on Behaviour, Morale and Performance

Under democratic leadership which can be said to be leadership through participation and consultation in decision making, the leader made all policies a matter of group discussion and decision, discussed the group goals in consultation with the group, suggested alternatives from which a choice could be made, allowed members to choose work partners and to divide up their work as they wished. The leader further tried to be objective and factual in giving criticism to the group. In a nutshell, a democratic leader involves subordinates in decision making process by soliciting their inputs and sharing ideas with them to arrive at a decision.

Employment of democratic type of leadership on the group produced the individuals who were more satisfied, more creative, and capable of higher quality work output. They also developed better relations with their superiors and were more likely to continue working in their absence.

Authoritarian Style of Leadership and its Effects on Behaviour, Morale and Output

The authoritarian type of leadership entails the view that any form of consultation is a weakness and that the individual who is in a position of responsibility should have sole authority over the decisions that are to be made within the organization. So, the leader made decisions alone and told those under him what to do in the light of decisions made. The leader also determined policies, designed plans, including identification of the activities for the group, and individuals. The leader was subjective in giving praise and criticism to the group and individuals.

Under authoritarian style of leadership, group members showed great dependence on the leader. The members were hostile to each other. They also displayed aggressive behaviour and had a tendency of blaming each other. The quality of output was, however, higher under autocratic leadership compared to that of democratic one. But members in the group seemed to need continuous supervision in order to continue working.

Laissez-Faire Style of Leadership and its Effects on Behaviour and Output

The term Laissez-faire is a French phrase which literally means "leave well alone or to give a "free reign". Therefore, the use of laissez-faire style of leadership meant that, the leader in Lewin's research did not provide any policy to the group. Individuals or group were completely free to make decisions without consulting the leader. In laissez-faire type of leadership, there was no systematic planning. The leader was indifferent, uninvolved with the activities of the group or individuals and did not appraise what was happening to the group. The results of laissez-faire style of leadership showed that the group was disorganized. In addition, members of the group were dissatisfied and the output of the group was lowest compared to the groups that operated under democratic or authoritarian leaderships.

Investigations that have been carried out using Lewin's frame of reference in relation to leadership styles and particularly in African schools and classrooms reveal that the most commonly used style of leadership is authoritarian. Grindal (1972) observed that there was almost total absence of spontaneity among students of primary schools among the Sisala in Northern Ghana. Thus, teacher's entry into a classroom was followed by general silence, and the pupils stood up as a sign of respect. Lessons involved little or no discussion. The teacher asked questions; pupils hurriedly browsed through their books and then raised their hands up if they found the correct answer. The teacher then invited one of the pupils to respond to the question. The pupil stood up and while still looking down, he responded to the question. If the teacher was not satisfied with the answer, he did not address the question to another pupil. Instead, he provided the answer and occasionally ridiculed the pupil.

Grindal attributed the authoritarian and the rigidity of the classroom atmosphere among Sisala to socio-cultural factors. In most African societies, authority of the elders was unquestioned. Given that teachers are older than pupils, they are not in a position to be challenged by pupils. Moreover, school education in many African countries is examination oriented. Thus, there is a prevalent tendency for teachers to drill pupils with facts for reproduction in examinations. The students in turn are not interested in the process of learning and qualification or mastery of skills and knowledge. Instead, they appear concerned about being certified, for a good certificate may ensure a good job and a place in higher institutions of learning (Dore, 1975). This approach to learning gives little room to problem solving oriented learning and discussions. Instead, it encourages mechanical and rote learning to which Freire (1972) referred as "the banking concept of education". The resultant outputs of mechanical learning is reproduction of information almost verbatim as it was given by the teacher. One of the major shortcomings of mechanical learning is that, it stunts understanding and creativity in learners.

Authoritarian atmosphere is most prevalent in many African schools and it is very effective in instilling fear of authority in pupils. Indeed, the classroom arrangement whereby all pupils sit in rows of desks facing the teacher enhances the authority of the teacher. This seating arrangement makes it almost impossible for pupils to interact. Manase and Kisanga (1978) said that pupils are made to sit in such a way that "each face speaks to the back of another pupils' head. Continued exposure to authoritarian type of learning situation therefore breeds a feeling of helplessness, worthlessness and inadequacy among pupils. As a consequence, students became over dependent on the teacher and others in positions of authority.

To produce independent thinkers, problem solving and creative people, schools must encourage democratic style of leadership. This approach of leadership recognizes that pupils and adults learn better when they participate in the learning process.

Teaching Methods and their Influence on Teacher-Pupil Interactions in the Classroom

There are different methods of teaching which a teacher can use. These methods have varying effects on the pupil's participation in the learning process. Flanders (1970) identified two types of teachers, namely, direct and indirect teachers. Flanders assessed the amount and quality of teacher-pupil contact in the classroom via verbal behaviour to arrive at these categories of teachers. According to Flanders, direct teachers have the following characteristics:

(i) They employ lecturing approach in the classroom, that is, they give facts or opinions about content or procedures. They also express their own ideas.
(ii) They give students directions, commands or orders to which pupils are expected to comply with.
(iii) Direct teachers are said to be fond of justifying authority, and also go to great lengths to explain why they do what they do.

On the whole, direct teachers give pupils little or no opportunities for participation in the classroom. The teacher talks most of the time and she/he expects compliance from the pupils. There is hardly any

Fundamentals of Sociology of Education

interaction among pupils; there is instead a single channel of communication from the teacher to the class.

Indirect teachers on the other hand, employ multiple channels of communication. In this case, there exists teacher-pupil and pupil-pupil interaction. Some of the characteristics of this method are:

(i) They accept students' feelings and they use non-threatening tone to students.
(ii) They praise and encourage student action.
(iii) They also use humour in the classroom from time to time to diffuse tension.
(iv) They accept and use students' ideas, clarify, build and develop ideas suggested by students.
(v) They ask students questions about content or procedures as a means of encouraging and soliciting inputs from students.

Using Flanders categorization of teachers on basis of their interaction and teaching approaches, studies have been carried out to establish their effects on pupils' academic performance. The findings have been inconclusive. It is reported that pupils favour teachers who use indirect approach of interaction. Thus, they rate such teachers as significantly more effective than direct teachers. Indirect teachers seem to produce better test results than direct ones in Arithmetic in children of normal ability and of ages 6 to 9 and 11 to 12, Biology in ages 13 to 14, and problem solving in age group 12 to 13. However, indirect approach does not seem to produce good performance in pupils of age group 9 to 10 with high and low ability respectively in Science Principles.

The use of indirect approach does not also produce good performance in children with average ability of ages of 9 to 10. Other studies too, have not found any significant differences between direct and indirect approaches to teaching with respect to pupil outputs of ages 6 to 9 in reading accuracy and attainment in Physics.

Besides the direct and indirect ways of teaching and interacting with pupils, the teacher can also utilize learner-centred method and teacher centred approaches. Learner centred methods involve children in their learning. In this approach, the teacher acts as a facilitator and as a guide. But the teacher-centred approach to teaching is, teacher-dominated. The teacher acts as the only source or fountain of knowledge. Thus he/she zealously "pours" information, facts and opinions into pupils' minds. This approach seems to assume that pupils' minds are "empty".

These teacher-centred methods of teaching are very prevalent in less industrialised economies like Kenya. This may be explained by the fact that they require less resources and less preparation. Large proportions of teachers in less industrialised economies are untrained and ill-equipped to handle child-centred methods of teaching. Therefore, predominance of teacher-centred methods of teaching exists.

Child-centred approaches give students more opportunities to participate in their learning, though there is no conclusive evidence that they produce superior academic performance. However, Brophy and Good (1974) established that learner-centred approaches to teaching benefit divergent thinkers among students more than they benefit convergent thinkers because they are not confined to the syllabus. Such students are not very dependent on the teacher. On the other hand, convergent thinkers are more bound to the syllabus and more dependent on the teacher and therefore are more likely to benefit from teacher-centred methods of teaching.

Teacher Expectations and Students' Academic Performance

In Rosenthal and Jacobson's experiment of 1968, teachers were given the names of children in their class who were "expected" to show dramatic intellectual growth in the year ahead. Although these children were of average intelligence, teachers, were told that they had a lot of potential and thus they were expected to do well academically. Surprisingly, when these students were retested later, they were found to have made significant gain in intelligence-based tests in comparison to their classmates. Even though Rosenthal and Jacobson experiment has not been replicated in all cases, the influence of teachers' beliefs about the potential for change in performance cannot be ignored.

Burstall (1968), on the teaching of French in Britain among some primary schools found out that there was a significant relationship between high-scoring and low ability children and teachers' positive attitude towards them. Again, Keddie (1971) established that when students were streamed according to ability, teachers of low-ability students did not prepare for their lessons adequately and in addition tended to ignore pupils' questions. On the other hand, teachers of classes with high ability students were better prepared to teach and they also took questions asked by their students seriously even though the questions were similar to those asked by students in the low-ability class.

Grieger (1971) concluded that characteristics that appeared to influence teacher expectations include, socio-economic status as expressed in dress, style of speech, and ability as expressed in terms of prior academic performance. In respect to language, Bernstein (1971), noted that children from low socio-status background had language disabilities. They express themselves in what Bernstein described as restricted language code while those from middle and upper socio-economic backgrounds use elaborate language.

Becker (1952) and Kaplan (1952) in their respective studies noted that teachers interact differently with pupils of different socio-classes. Becker found out that teachers considered teaching lower socio-class children as unrewarding. Teachers were of the opinion that such children had low level of motivation. Further, teachers criticized such children for aggressive behaviour indiscipline, lack of cleanliness and what appeared to be children's indifference to hygiene.

Kaplan observed that teachers found the behaviour of children from low-social class disturbing and annoying. These children were associated with behaviours such as stealing, lying, cheating, aggression and destruction of property. Teachers also detested such children's inattentiveness, indifference to school work and non-conformity. In his study, Good Acre (1968) found out that teachers working in schools servicing children of low-socio-economic status tended to assume that they had no pupils of above average cognitive abilities. Teachers were dissatisfied with teaching children from low socio-economic status. Thus, a large proportion of teachers of children from low social class aspired to move to other schools compared to teachers of children from high social status.

Teacher and Classroom Management

The term management refers to the process of getting activities completed efficiently with and through other people. In the classroom situation, the teacher is the manager. The teacher, therefore, has the responsibility of harnessing the energies of pupils so that they can effectively acquire necessary knowledge skills and value systems that will help them to become productive members of the society. The teacher must guide the pupils to acquire proper conduct of behaviour for social living.

In carrying out these roles, the teacher may experience discipline problems. One of the reasons why disorders or deviancy occur in the classroom is because the classroom is a very artificial kind of place. For instance, children from various socio-economic backgrounds and with diverse intellectual endowments are brought together and are expected to learn through specified methods within the confinement of a single room. In such an unnatural situation, almost anything can go wrong. Farrant (1964) suggested that some of the most common disorders in the classroom originate from teachers' inability to exercise authority and unpreparedness to teach. Discipline problems can also emanate from lack of co-operation between other members of staff, parents and community in general.

Authority and Discipline

Authority is the ability to enforce obedience. Without authority, management of a classroom is bound to break down. To command respect and wield authority over pupils, a teacher must do the following:

Formulate Reasonable Rules

Harmony in the classroom is dependent on keeping rules. Such rules should outline the expected behaviour of pupils in the classroom. The rules should be reasonable and should be known to all pupils.

Moreover, such rules should specify how pupils for instance, should show their intention to respond to questions, handing in their written work, coming in and going out of the classroom.

Maintain Dignity

A teacher should not involved in unwarranted arguments or physical struggles with children. He/she should avoid trying to be popular with the children because this is likely to make the teacher not to demand that pupils adhere to the set out rules. A teacher should also set good examples to pupils through his words, actions and behaviour. For example, a teacher should dress up appropriately

Be Consistent

A teacher must be consistent in applying disciplinary measurers all the times. However, the punishment should be commensurate with the offence. Discipline should be applied to all without exceptions. Favouritism is often the cause of discipline problems.

Be Firm

The teacher's authority will be weakened if he/she appears to waiver on certain decisions. The teacher must make decisions after careful consideration and carry them out. Particularly, when beginning to teach a new class, teachers must establish their authority firmly. It is easier to relax his/her hold than to regain authority once it is lost. Disorder in the classroom should be tackled immediately; otherwise delay may be interpreted by pupils as a weakness. When a teacher promises to do something, she/he must carry it out otherwise the children will not be able to take what the teacher says seriously.

Be Self-Critical

To ensure that authority prevails, the teacher must be able to reflect on his strong and weak points. This way, the teacher is able to give better guidance. A teacher must also avoid some forms of mannerism that might reduce his authority such as crying in front of the children, biting one's finger nails and other forms of emotional outbursts.

To maintain authority, teachers must strive to cultivate good relations with other members of staff, parents of the pupils and members of the community at large. These people interact with pupils and if the teachers' demands of discipline are not congruent with those of other stakeholders, their authority may be undermined. In the recent past, for instance, some parents in Kenya have beaten up teachers under the pretext that their demands on children are unreasonable.

Efficiency

A teacher must prepare well for all lessons, be methodical, that is, the lesson must be logically organized; and must have all items needed during the teaching time. Poor teaching too, is the major cause of discipline. Poor teaching may arise from teacher's failure to prepare properly for the lessons in terms of content and presentation. If the material prepared for instance, is beyond the understanding of children or not challenging enough, children will lose interest and are likely to become restless and noisy. A lesson may also be boring because the children are not involved in the learning due to lack of teaching aids. All the human senses of touch, sight, hearing, smell and taste should be engaged in the learning process. Teaching aids help to bring to use all these senses in the learning process.

Success in learning is one of the most valuable weapons against disorder in the classroom. Success breeds success and is a confidence builder. The teacher, therefore, must prepare for lessons properly, and involve the pupils in the learning process. Busy pupils will have very little time for mischief. Again, the teacher must observe punctuality. Children often make noise and cause trouble when the teacher is late for class.

When students were asked to state the qualities they liked in teachers, they said that they preferred friendly and helpful teachers to teachers who frequently scolded them or used sarcasm. Davison and Lang (1960-61) found out that those teachers' who had positive feelings about the children they taught boosted pupils' self-image, academic achievement and desirable behaviour.

Interaction Dynamics in the Classroom

In dealing with the dynamics of the classroom, we shall examine how pupils' characteristics such as *intellectual ability, social background, physical attractiveness, their behaviour* and *sex* affect their interaction with their teachers. We shall also explore how pupils interact among themselves.

Actual or perceived *academic performance* of a pupil seems to influence pupil interaction with the teacher. Brophy and Good (1974) pointed out that teachers generally preferred high achieving students who were hardworking, dependable and responsive to independent students who aggressively pursued their own interests. Mcpherson (1972) concurred that teachers appeared to believe that docility and effort among students equalled success. She observed that a successful student who was neither docile nor hardworking was seen as a threat to teachers' belief-system. As a result, teachers often minimized or even disbelieved such students' performance. Teachers' concept of a good pupil, therefore, appear to be characterized by docility, attentiveness and lack of intellectual independence. Teachers also interact differently with pupils of various intellectual ability. Brophy and Good (1974) said that teachers respond differently to student's failure. Some teachers geared their instruction primarily towards high achievers. However, while some teachers spend more time with low-achievers, they give them less approval. Little or no approval to students may de-motivate them, thus neutralising teachers' efforts.

Socio-economic status of a pupil is another variable that has been found to influence the quality and quantity of teacher-pupil interaction. McPherson (1974) found out that teachers were closer to students who belonged to the same socio-economic status as themselves. In her study on rural school teachers of solidly lower-middle-class, she found out that teachers had clear preference for pupils of similar background as themselves as opposed to those from the working and the upper middle classes. She observed that the teachers knew exactly who belonged where and used this information both in interpreting behaviour and in deciding how to handle it. It has also been noted that many of the *low achieving students* come from lower social status. Further, studies have shown that teachers under-estimate the ability of working class pupils. Some teachers have often inaccurately assumed that slow and less likeable children come from poor homes. In case of *bad behaviour*, teachers are on the whole more tolerant of *physically attractive pupils* they approved of.

With regard *to gender*, it has been established that teachers treat girls differently from boys. A study by Sadker and Sadker (1985) found out that teachers gave more attention to boys than girls and were more likely to carry on an extended conversation with boys than with girls. In many situations, girls are often not given feedback about their performance. The result is that many girls go through their education surrounded by unresponsive silence about what effect, if any, of their actions or contributions has.

Thus, girls go through their education without sufficient information about the quality of their work. Moreover, textbooks used in the classrooms enhance silence by girls and their invisibility. The images of females are under represented compared to their male counterparts. Van Scotter, et.al, (1991) observed that the character traits of male students portrayed in textbooks are ingenuity, creative, bravery, perseverance, achievement, adventurousness, helpfulness, acquisition of skills, competitiveness, use of power, autonomy, self-respect and friendship. On the other hand, girls are associated with attributes such as dependency, passivity, incompetence, fearfulness, concern about physical appearance, obedience and domesticity. Because of differential treatment of boys and girls by teachers, it is not surprising that girls are out-performed by boys in academic pursuits even when they happen to have more potential than boys. This is in conformity with the labelling theory, whereby individuals so labelled "live up" to the labels assigned to them.

Language is also a key to interaction dynamics in the classroom. The success of a learner in acquiring knowledge, skills and values in order to become a productive member of the society is dependent to a large extent on the teacher's ability to communicate with a learner of different linguistic abilities and language backgrounds. Bernestein (1971) observed that children bring with them to school linguistic problems. Therefore, such children have limited powers of language communication. He continued to note that while children of different linguistic backgrounds were likely to adapt to each others mode of communication; there was a possibility that teachers would experience communication problems with learners. It is postulated that young people have a greater need to communicate with each other if only to keep information from the ear of "apparently" dominant authority of the teacher.

Omondi (1999), acknowledged an emergence of a new language in the linguistic ecology of Kenya called" sheng" (particularly among the urban youth). This language has helped youth from different linguistic backgrounds to communicate without being understood by the older generation. Given that teachers by virtue of age form a class of their own and also that they come from different socio-economic and linguistic backgrounds from those of learners, we may assume that they will experience problems communicating with learners who have already "overcome" theirs by developing communication codes among themselves.

In Kenya, language communication problems between teachers and learners may further be aggravated by the fact that English (a medium of instruction in schools) is a second language for the teachers and students. Omondi (1999) has noted that there are forty Kenyan African languages or mother tongues. Each one of these languages is associated with a particular tribe. People of a particular tribe infuse their mother-tongue mode of speaking into English. Thus, there is a high probability that teachers of one ethnic community have difficulties communicating with learners whose mother-tongues are different from theirs.

On the interaction among pupils, sociologists have studied this phenomenon and have developed a sociometry technique. Sociometry refers to measurement of social behaviour of groups. Sociometry technique constitutes a sociometric test. This is a device by which data is collected for studying the structure of a group. The information gathered is used to shed some light on the relationship between members of a group. These relationships may be based on attraction and repulsion and indifference of members in the group. In the application of a sociometry technique, each member of a group/classroom is requested to indicate the members of the group they would like to associate with for a given activity or occasion. The members are also asked to mention if there are any other members in the group they would prefer not to be with for that activity. To get an objective picture of the structure of the group, sociometrists usually ask members of the group to make their choices in private.

The results of sociometric tests tend to produce "stars", "isolates" and "neglectees". Stars are those members of the group who are over chosen. These individuals are likely to assume leadership more easily than isolates and neglectees. While a "star" is over chosen by the members of the either group, an isolate is one who neither chooses nor is chosen by anyone. A neglectee on the other hand, is an individual who chooses others for a given activity but she or he is not chosen by anyone in the group. Once the results of a sociometric test are collated, an objective picture of the group emerges. On the basis of these results, the socio-metrist can suggest measures influencing group dynamics and give solutions to the problems that the group faces in the process of interaction.

Thus, interaction dynamics in the classroom are likely to be determined by a variety of factors. These factors include student's academic ability, athletic prowess, socio-economic background, similarity in behaviour, affiliation to the same clubs, religion, physical attractiveness, ethnicity, same locality, sex, and age. Any of these factors individually and or in combination with others seem to determine interaction patterns. For instance, pupils of the same academic ability tend to be attracted towards each other. Similarly, students gifted in athletic prowess seem to share similar interests.

Summary

The chapter began by identifying the characteristics of the classroom, the principal ones being that it refers to a group of pupils who are more or less of the same age and in the same grade or class within the school system. It then examined the interaction patterns between teachers and pupils through different leadership styles and approaches in teaching. It also examined the influence of the teachers' expectations on academic performance and their role in classroom management.

With respect to leadership styles, it emerged that democratic style is better than authoritarian or laissez-faire because it produces more creative and dependable individuals. Authoritarian leadership tended to foster aggressive, competitive students requiring constant supervision to sustain work while lasses-faire produced disorganised and directionless behaviour. Similarly, democratic or pupil-centred methods fostered problem solving approach and creativity compared to teacher-centred methods of teaching. The influence of teachers' expectations on students' performance is found to be critical.

Generally, pupils who are expected to perform well by teachers, usually do so. Such pupils work extra hard in order to live up to the expectations of their teachers. Finally, the chapter looked at the role of the teacher in classroom management. This review revealed that teachers who prepare for their teaching and apply reasonable classroom rules to their students have minimal classroom problems.

Study Questions

1. Explain the relationship between different types of leadership styles and the student's academic performance and behaviour.

2. Using examples, explain the extent to which teacher expectations influence students' academic performance and behaviour.

3. Discuss the causes of discipline problems in the classroom. Suggest ways of avoiding them.

4. Discuss the determinants of interaction dynamics between teachers and students and among students.

References

Bernstein, Bail. (1961). Social Structure, Language and Learning. *British Journal of Educational Research*, VIII, June.

Mackenzie, Liz. (1993). *On Our Feet: Taking Steps to Challenge Women's Oppression.* Belville, South Africa. CACE Publications.

Gakuru, N. O. (1977). *Pre-Primary and Assess to Educational Opportunities in Nairobi.* Nairobi: Institute of Development Studies, IDS/W.P/138.

Morrison, A., and Mclutyre, D. (1971). *Schools And Socialization*, Manchester: C. Nicholls and Company.

Somerset, H.C.A. (1974). A Survey of Fourth Form Pupils on Educational and Occupational Expectations. In Court and Dharam, *Education Society and development. New Perspectives from Kenya.* Nairobi: Oxford University Press.

10

Gender and Education

Concept of Gender and Sex

The term gender is widely used to differentiate between men and women on socially designed constructs rather than biological differences. Sex signifies the physical, biological and genetic variations between females and males. It refers to whether individuals are born with female or male genitalia. Sex variations are innate while gender ones are socially constructed. Gender differences represent expectations people have of someone who is female or male.

Gender differentiation and its oppressive tendencies especially on the girl-child and women start right from birth. From the time babies are born, people treat boys and girls differently. Some African traditional cultures had special ways of announcing the sex of the newly born baby. For example, in the Kikuyu traditional culture, the birth of a boy was announced by the attendant with *five* ululations and that of a girl with *four*. Other comments that were made and are still being made when a baby boy is born include: a soldier, a warrior or a ruler is born. When a girl is born, the comments would be: gifts of beer, cows and goats have "come". The remarks about the birth of a baby girl are made in the expectation she will become a woman and on marriage, her bride groom will bring beer, goats, cows and other material objects as dowry to her parents in the traditional way of validating and sealing the marriage.

It is not surprising then, that different behaviour is expected from boys and girls in anticipation of the performance of the roles designated for them by the society. We note, therefore, *"wanja kahii"* a term among the Kikuyu culture given to a girl who acts as a boy and likes activities outside the domestic sphere, while the term *"huni wangechi'* is associated with a boy who behaves like a girl. According to this societal prescription, girls are expected to develop feminine qualities that best fit them into a domesticated home life while boys are supposed to acquire masculine traits for activities outside the home domain.

The above illustration indicates the expectations of society of how real women and real men should behave. Thus, while sex or biological variations are natural, gender variations are social constructs. The traditional African society expects women to cook, fetch water and firewood and care for the children. Furthermore, the society expects women to do more work than men. According to United Nations statistics, women perform 67 per cent of the world's working hours (Mackenzie, 1991). There are gender roles that can be changed. For example, men can easily bottle-feed the baby, fetch water, firewood, cook for the family, wash dishes, clothes and take care of children. This, however, rarely happens. Division of labour between males and females is strongly socially determined and is passed on to the successive generations through socialization. Socialization is so thorough that gender roles are viewed as innate and genetic origin is often used to explain gender variations.

Other gender constructed stereotypes concern mental acuity, physical prowess, and emotional stamina. It is generally perceived that intellect and all its attributes, such as rationality, logic and creativity are male qualities. Females are alleged to be illogical, emotional and not bright. None of these allegations have been proven beyond any doubt. Perhaps the reason why girls do not do well as their male counterparts is because they are not given equal opportunities to develop their capabilities. Throughout the history of the human race, females have been disadvantaged in all aspects of human endeavour because their "existence" has been viewed as auxiliary to men. As a result, women have been treated as inferior to men and have had less power to make decisions affecting themselves and communities. They have had little access to and control of material and non-material resources such as land and capital, skills and knowledge.

The Ideology of Sexism

Ideology here refers to sets of beliefs and visions about men and women that cannot be backed with facts. The term sexism refers to any form of discrimination shown to individuals because of their sex. The ideology of sexism argues that the female sex is weaker compared to male sex. In reality though, some females are stronger than males.

Sexist ideology is oppressive to both sexes. For instance, a man who is weak and is expected to perform as well as other strong men may get frustrated. A man who is the head of a family but has no means of providing material welfare for his wife and children feels the weight of societal expectations. Similarly, a man who feels the urge to release tension by crying but cannot also because it is not manly to do so, may result to other ways of releasing tension, for instance alcoholism. On the whole, sexist ideology still affects females more than males.

Gender Disparity in Education

There is documented evidence that female education is one of the most important forces of development (King, 1991). While it is important to educate both females and males, Forum for African Women Educationist (FAWE) enumerates a number of reasons in favour of educating the girl child. These are:

- It is a basic human right.
- It promotes gender equity.
- Educating girls is a better investment than boys' education because it has the highest return investment in the developing countries; it has multiplier effects, and empowers women to bring about other necessary changes like smaller family size, increased income, and non-market productivity.

Although it is agreed that educating females brings more benefits to society than educating males, more males and especially in less industrialized economies of Africa, continue to go to school and work their way up the educational ladder (Mueller, 1990). Thus, women who constitute half of humankind, unfortunately form 2/3 of the world's illiterates (Mackenzie, 1992:34). In Africa, 64% of illiterates are women (Ballara, 1992:6). In Kenya, over 60 percent of women are illiterate (Ministry of Planning and National Development, Literacy Survey, 1988). Most societies worldwide prefer to educate boys to girls and this is particularly so for poor families. An analysis of enrolment figures of students in the Kenyan educational system from pre-primary to university reveals wide disparities especially at secondary and post-secondary institutions.

Enrolment in Pre-Primary Schools

Pre-primary education caters for children aged 3-6 years. Generally, local communities and parents are responsible for establishing and running pre-schools. They provide land and physical facilities, pay the salaries of teachers, cater for feeding programmes, provide books and toys. Thus, though this sector has been expanding over the years, it has not expanded as much as other levels of the educational system due to minimal government involvement. The majority of children who attend pre-primary are those whose parents are wealthy and can pay exorbitant fees charged in privately run kindergartens, day care centres or nursery schools located in major urban centres. In 2002, the enrolment in pre-primary stood at 1,175,223. Girls accounted for 49.1% of the total enrolment (Republic of Kenya, Economic Survey, 2003). The enrolment of girls at pre-primary level is very encouraging; it has almost equalled that of boys. However, it should be noted that only 35% of the children in pre-primary group have an opportunity to attend pre-primary education.

Enrolment in Primary Schools

In 1963, when Kenya attained its independence, there were a total of 892,000 pupils in primary schools, 34% of whom were girls (Republic of Kenya, 1989-1993 Development Plan). Enrolment of girls in primary schools has continued to rise though it has not equalled that of boys. For instance, in 2000, there were 6,371.2 million children in primary schools. Girls accounted for (49.3%) of the total enrolment (Republic of Kenya, 2003). The increase in enrolment of girls at this level of education is encouraging but it is observed that only 35% of girls who enrol actually complete primary school compared with 55% for boys (Republic of Kenya, Development Plan 1997-2001). This is explained by higher drop-out rate for girls after standard 4 resulting from socio-economic and biological factors which shall be discussed later.

Enrolment in Secondary Schools

With respect to secondary school education, there has been remarkable rise in student enrolment. In 1963, the enrolment stood at about 30,000 students. The proportion of girls in secondary schools was 32% and has risen steadily to 47.2% by 2002 (Republic of Kenya, Economic Survey, 2002).

Gender gap in education in secondary schools at national level is slight. However, there are large imbalances in enrolment of girls at regional level. The provinces with the largest gender disparities include North Eastern with the percentage girls attending secondary education standing at 15.2%, Nairobi 40.1%, Western 44.2% Nyanza 42.4% and Coast 44.7% (Ministry of Education Statistics section l996). But in Central Province, girls have outstripped boys in enrolment at secondary school level.

Enrolment in Post-Secondary Educational Institutions

The low enrolment of girls in secondary schools has its continued effects on female education at university and other post-secondary educational institutions. Out of 62,875 students at public universities in 2001/2002 academic year, females constituted 32.7%. Again, in other post secondary learning institutions, female enrolment was lower in Primary Teacher Training Colleges. They accounted for 47.4% out of a total enrolment of 45,730 in 2000/2001.Female representation in polytechnics was low; it constituted 30.2% of total students enrolment. Male student continued to dominate in Technical Training Institutes and Institutes of Technology where male students in 2001/2002 academic years constituted 55% and 45% respectively.

Adult Education

Adult education plays an important role in giving functional literacy to over 30 percent of females who are illiterate. This kind of education, however, does not form part of the regular educational system.

According to Republic of Kenya (2003:51), there are currently 114,865 persons enrolled in adult literacy classes. In the year 2000, there were 93,903 persons enrolled. However, adult literacy enrolments have dropped drastically from 415,000 students in 1979 to 109,929 students in 2005 (Republic of Kenya, 2003). Table 1 presents adult education enrolment by sex from 1998-2002.

Table I: Adult Education Enrolment by Sex 1998 – 2004

Year	Male	Female	Total	% of Female Enrolment
1998	26,180	74,081	0,261	73.9
1999	30,200	71, 06l	101,261	70.2
2000	25,802	68,101	93,903	72.5
2001	26,479	66,573	93,903	72.0
2002	41,341	73,524	114,865	64.0
2003	31,305	77,126	108,431	71.1
2004	31,512	78,411	109,929	71.3

Source: Republic of Kenya, Economic Survey, 2005

The data in Table I show that there are more women enrolled for adult literacy classes than men. This is explained by the fact that there are more illiterate women than men. For instance, l999 population census revealed that 60% illiterate adults in Kenya are women (Republic of Kenya, 1999, Housing Population Census) literacy. Highest rates of illiterates were and still are in the major pastoralist areas (Waithaka, 1992:139).

Information presented so far clearly shows that there is gender disparity in education. Besides this disparity, there is evidence that boys perform better than girls in almost all subjects at natural examinations.(Government of Kenya and United Nations Children's Fund, 1992:l03 and l06). For instance, in the 2001 results of Kenya Primary Certificate of Education (KCPE) boys did better than girls in Mathematics, Science, Geography, History, Civics, Religious Education, English and Kiswahili objective questions. Out of the 800 top student performers at Kenya Secondary Certificate of Education in 2001, there were 270 girls constituting 33.75% (Waheinya Kariuki, 2001). The questions are: Why are there fewer girls compared to that of boys at almost all levels of Kenya's educational system? Why do girls perform poorly academically in relation to boys?

Factors that Affect the Education of Girls

1. The society sees educating of boys more important than that of girls. Families who cannot easily afford to send both sons and daughters to school, therefore, view financial return on the girls' education investments as less rewarding than that of boys. The argument is that girls will eventually leave their parents when they get married and therefore, their education is seen as a financial asset to the in-laws rather than the biological parents.

2. The society does not put a lot of emphasis on the education of girls. It is argued that a woman does not need to be educated because, unlike the man who is the head of a family and bread earner, she is expected to be a wife, a home maker and a mother. She is seen as a provider of the non-material services to her family such as to love, care and nurturing children while the husband sustains the family materially. This practice ignores the fact that over 30% of families worldwide, Kenya included, are now headed by women (Mackenzie 1993 and Republic of Kenya, 1997-2001 Development Plan). Furthermore, a good proportion of women who are married have irresponsible husbands.

3. There is a belief held by members of the society especially among men that, educated women are less "feminine" and are not easily

controlled by men. This is because education enables such women to become materially independent of men.

4. Sometimes, girls drop out because of pregnancies. In Kenya, over 10,000 secondary school girls drop out on account of pregnancy every year (Government of Kenya and UNICEF 1992). Another problem is early marriage among girls. Matters pertaining to marriage in Kenya are governed by different laws which are recognized by the constitution. There are four systems of marriage in Kenya: these are Customary Law, Moslem Law, Hindu Law and Civil Law, which embodies the English philosophy of life and Christian doctrine. Civil and Hindu systems of marriage recognise monogamous marriage while customary law and Moslem Laws recognize polygamous marriage. Customary law allows a man to marry as many wives as he wishes, while Islamic law allows four wives at any given time. Statutory law provides for a monogamous marriage. Under the marriage Acts, the man and woman must have attained the age of 18 years. Under Hindu law, the bridegroom must have attained the age of 18 years and the bride 16 years. If the bride is between 16 and 18 years, the consent of a guardian or the High Court must be sought. Thus, under the Hindu marriage law, girls who have not attained the age of marriage can enter into marriage. Such girls (if they were going to school) will have only completed the second year of secondary education.

With regard to some customary laws, capacity to contract marriage is often linked to circumcision and puberty. Puberty may be attained as early as 9 or 11 years, which in effect, means that a child could enter into a contract of marriage before she/he is eighteen years of age. This is particularly true for girls. Indeed, early marriages are common in some parts of Kenya such as, the Coast, North Eastern, and some parts of the Rift Valley province.

5. Girls drop out school because they cannot cope with the pressure of school work and domestic chores. Girls are overburdened with household duties, such as fetching water and firewood, washing clothes and dishes, taking care of their siblings and other household related jobs. These activities rob girls of adequate time

Gender and Education

to study and as a result, perform poorly at school, eventually some losing interest and quitting school.

6. The majority of girls especially at secondary level attend poorly equipped and under staffed secondary schools. For example, in 1986 there were 635 Government maintained schools and 1,497 harambee schools (355 of the latter were unaided); 47% of the girls' schools were not government maintained compared to 35% of the boys school (Government of Kenya and UNICEF, 1989). Though current data on this issue is unavailable, it is still likely that the situation has not changed much. This situation may lead to serious drop out, as students see little chance for academic success. Out of 18 national secondary schools, only 7 are boarding schools for girls, while boys have 9 such secondary schools. The other 2 secondary schools are co-educational (The Kenya National Council, 1996). There is evidence that co-educational secondary schools are not good for girls. Girls are likely to suffer from sexual harassment from their male counterparts (Mackenzie, 1993).

7. Most of the secondary schools attended by girls are either day or co-educational schools. Day secondary schools do not provide students with good learning environment especially girls. While at home, girls devote more of their time doing household chores rather than school work

8. Girls receiving education from co-educational schools and especially boarding ones encounter sexual harassment from both their colleagues and the male teachers. Mackenzie (1993) recounts what she calls a "night of madness", when 271 teenage girls were attacked by their male counterparts. As a result of the attack, 19 girls died and 71 were raped. Sexual harassment may have contributed to poor performance of girls in academic work and loss of interest in school. Loss of interest in schoolwork may result in school drop out. Kibera (1993) found out that girls in co-educational secondary schools have extremely low educational and career aspirations compared to girls attending unisexual secondary schools. Indeed, girls in unisexual secondary schools had higher educational and career aspirations compared to male

students attending similar institutions. Unisexual secondary schools are generally well-equipped and staffed with the majority of teachers of the same sex to the gender of the students. Such girls' secondary schools have similar facilities and human resources with those of boys. It is not surprising then that girls educated in quality secondary schools perform as well as boys and at times, even better than boys. The examination results of Kenya Secondary Certificate of Education of 1993 attest to this (Standard Newspaper, 23rd February, 1994). This excellent performance of girls is mainly attributed to the conducive learning environment girls enjoy in unisexual secondary schools free of sexual harassment and overburdening household chores.

The marginalisation of girls in the educational arena leads to the marginalisation in the labour market. High rewarding occupations are awarded to those with most education and therefore, most women are automatically excluded from such jobs on the account of having little or no formal school education.

Gender and the Hidden Curriculum

Hidden curriculum comprises unwritten purposes of education. It refers to the informal experiences pupils obtain by picking up information omitted by teachers, school personnel, and pupils as well as exposure to the school organization and learning materials. Letzotte, et.al (1980) defined hidden curriculum as norms, beliefs and attitudes reflected in the school practices and the behaviour of teachers, students and the school community at large. The formal curriculum on the other hand, refers to the courses that are taught at various levels of the school system. Often, the hidden curriculum produces different outcomes for girls and boys due to a number of reasons.

It has been observed that teachers' behaviour can result in significant difference in women's educational experiences from those of men despite attending the same institutions, sharing the same classrooms and being taught by the same teachers. Sadker and Sadker (1985) found out that teachers pay more attention to boys than girls. For instance, teachers hold longer conversation with boys than with girls.

Even when teachers speak to girls, they did not give them the same kind of feedback as boys. In addition, they found that the reaction to boys was often dynamic, precise and effective while reaction to girls was often unstimulating and unfocused. Thus, girls seem to go through the education process without sufficient information about the quality of their work and without confirmation that their presence is felt.

Teachers expect different characteristics from girls and boys and these expectations in turn produce different educational outcomes. Teachers expect girls to be appreciative, calm, conscientious, co-operative, mannerly, dependable and mature while they expect boys to be active, adventurous, aggressive, assertive, curious, energetic, inventive, enterprising and independent. Effective learning requires learners to be curious and aggressive in the learning process. It is not, therefore, surprising that boys do better than girls in school because teachers expect them to do so.

Girls' problems in schools are compounded by the fact that textbooks perpetuate male dominance. Books used in schools on the whole portray a male dominated world. Obura with a team of researchers (1991) made an in-depth examination of school books used in Kenya's primary schools (Mathematics, Sciences, Technical, Language and Social Science books) and recorded two major findings. These were:

- Images of females were considerably fewer in number than images of males.
- The few images of females in the text books were negative in relation to the images of males. It was noted that had the few female images been striking, powerful and positive they would arguably have had a strong and positive impact despite their less frequency. An approximation of percentage of male and female appearance in textbooks is presented in table II.

The scarcity of female images as well as lack of positive ones in text books and other reading materials may lead girls to feel insignificant, inferior and to lose interest in learning. Females are associated with house chores, taking care of children and the family. These roles in Kenya are not perceived to require education

Language is another instrument which is used to marginalise women. This is because language is a powerful tool in establishing the meaning of our experience. It enables us to interpret and organize the world through our senses. The language used in the textbooks, and forms of print and electronic media, is male dominated. For example, we often speak of forefathers rather than ancestors, mankind instead of humankind, chairman rather than chairperson, manpower rather than human resources or personnel. Use of male specific words rather than neutral ones marginalises and silences females.

Table II: Percentage of Appearance of Males and Females in Textbooks

Textbook	Percentage of Appearance males vis-à-vis female	
	Males	Females
Mathematics Book 3	71.7	28.3
Mathematics Book 6	92.9	7.1
Mathematics Book 8	82.6	17.1
Agriculture	76.9	7.6
Science/Technical Books	93.3	7.7
Social Science	92.1	7.9

Source: Obura A. P. (1991). Changing Images Nairobi: ACTS

To counteract the negative effects of the hidden curriculum on the education of girls, measures should be taken to strengthen and expand research on gender issues on classroom interaction, among teachers, boys and girls, school practices, such as the use of playing grounds by boys and girls, value attached to boys' and girls' sports and games respectively, structure, for example prefect selection and staffing hierarchy. The results of these studies are likely to help teachers and education policy makers diversify the curriculum.

Gender, Education and Employment Opportunities

The majority of women in Africa work in the agricultural sector (Wichterich Christa, 1985). Agricultural work is demanding and underpaid and is usually done by the unschooled. According to the Republic of Kenya Economic Survey, (2003), there were 503.4 females (29.6%) in wage employment out of 1,699.7regular employees in 2002. Of the female wage earners, Education sector remained the major female employer with a share of 27.1 % of the total female employment. The proportion of females employed in industries traditionally dominated by males such as building and construction industry, quarrying, mining electricity and water, are very low. It has also been established that women's average earnings are only 46 percent of men's (Sebstad, 1992).

Additionally, majority of women including the educated ones do not own property; family property is usually registered in the husband's name. Consequently, most women are not able to secure loans for economic enterprises because they lack the collateral securities required by financial institutions. Without education and property, women have no access to resources.

Outcomes of Under-Representation of Female Student at all Levels of Kenya's Educational System

According to the Kenya's Ministry of Planning and National Development, (1988) an overall adult literacy rate was 54 percent with female literacy lagging at 40 percent. Since then, the literacy rate for females has steadily improved. Currently, it stands at 70% while that of males is 86.3% (hhttp://www.hmnet.com/Africa/Kenya/Kenya.html,07/02/2007).

The under-representation of girls and women in educational institutions means that:

- Women and girls are denied their human right to education which in turn means that women are bound to be silent because

they do not have a language to express their needs, interest and concerns.
- Women are not equipped with occupational skills. As a result, they are not able to access financially high rewarding employment. Women lack management and entrepreneurial skills to assist them in self employment. The majority of women in Kenya and their children therefore, live in poverty.
- Women are unprepared to care of their health and nutritional needs including those of their families. Socio-cultural practices demand that female take care of homes, children and the entire family.
- Women are excluded from decision making positions and politics, partly because they lack education and also due to socio-cultural beliefs that view leadership and politics as male activities.

Some Ways of Improving the Educational, Occupational, and Leadership Chances of Women

- Because of the links between education and the economy, Kenyan women are marginalized in all wage employment sectors of the Kenyan economy. This is further aggravated by the fact that whether women have received education or not, they are still marginalized due to the ingrained social cultural beliefs that women are unequal to men. But, in spite of socio-cultural beliefs education of women remains the key to socio-economic and political emancipation.
- As more women receive formal and higher education, they acquire more skills and expertise needed in various fields of development. Educated women will become more aware of issues, more adaptable to change and less passive to their conditions.
- Towards this goal, world organizations, governments, communities, non-government organizations and women organizations must give top priority to the education of girls. More bursaries should be specifically set up for girls from poor

families. When this happens, poor families may refrain from withdrawing girls from schools on account of lack of school fees.
- Members of society at large and especially parents and teachers must be sensitized on the importance of educating girls through the radio, public lectures and songs.
- More research should be carried out in schools and in the communities in order to establish the relative importance of the factors that impinge on the education of girls.
- Comprehensive data on the situation of girls and women with particular reference to poor urban, poor rural, nomadic, school dropouts, and adolescent mothers should be compiled to facilitate appropriate planning.
- Confidence and capacity building-skill sessions should be organized for women and girls. Households, especially those headed by women should be assisted in starting and sustaining income-generating activities so that they are empowered to cater for the material needs of their families.
- A vigorous career education counselling for girls should be introduced in schools to enlighten them on career options that exist, and their academic requirements particularly for Science subjects and mathematics. Girls do very poorly in these subjects. If this counselling is not carried out, women will continue to aspire for jobs such as teaching, nursing and secretarial work that are traditionally associated with women.
- Since girls drop out of schools due to pregnancies, serious campaigns to educate girls about their sexuality and how to deal with teenage relationships should form part of the school curriculum from the upper primary classes onwards. A large proportion of women from primary to university have had their education interrupted and sometimes ended due to teenage pregnancy.
- Adult education which has been in the decline, should be revitalized to cater for vast numbers of illiterate women.
- A bi-annual publication on the status of the education of girls should be launched. Additionally, Gender studies should be offered in all institutions of teacher education.

- Educational materials and textbooks that portray girls and women only in their traditional roles should be rewritten in order to provide more balanced role models.

Summary

The review of educational status of women in Kenya has shown that women have been outstripped by men at all levels of the education system and especially at the post-secondary level. To ignore the education of women who constitute the majority, is to hamper the country's development. Education of women should be given priority. To achieve this, intervention measures such as bursaries, establishment of quality unisexual boarding secondary schools, career education and sex education should be provided for girls. The society at large should be sensitised about the importance of education of girls and women and its overall impact on the development of the society. Finally, research on the effect of the hidden curriculum on the educational chances of both females and males should be carried out.

Study Questions

1. Using examples from your community, explain the concepts of sex and gender and their impact on the education of girls.

2. Critically examine the factors that influence the education of girls and boys in your community.

3. Using examples, explain how gender parity in education can be achieved

References

East African Standard. (1994). Precious Blood Tops in `O' Level Exams. Nairobi *Standard Newspaper,* 23rd February.

Forum for African Women Educationalists (Undated). *Girls' Education.* Nairobi: FAWE Government of Kenya and United Nations Children's Fund (1989). *Situation Analysis of Children and Women in Kenya,* Nairobi: UNICEF, Kenya.

_____. (1992). *Children and Women in Kenya. A situation Analysis:* Nairobi; Kenya

Hazlewood, A. (1979). *The Economy of Kenya, The Kenyatta Era,* New York: Oxford University Press.

Kamotho, J. (1996). School Entrants drop: Enrolment down by 13 percent. *Daily Nation.* Nairobi: Tuesday 16th July.

Kenya National Examination Council. (1996). *List of National Secondary Schools.* Nairobi: Kenya National Examination Council.

King, Elizabeth. (1991). Wide Benefits Seen From Improved Education for Women". *Washington Economic Reports:* Nairobi. United States Information Agency, No.4.

Lezotte, L. et.al. (1980). *School Learning Climate and Student Achievement.* Lansing: Michigan State University

Mackenzie, Liz. (1993). *On Our Feet, Taking Steps to Challenge Women's Oppression.* Bellville: South Africa. CACE Publications.

Ministry of Planning and National Development. (1988). *Kenya Rural Literacy Survey, 1988: Basic Report.* Nairobi: Central Bureau of Statistics

Ministry of Education Science and Technology. (1996). Boys and Girls enrolled in Kenya by Province in Kenya. Nairobi: Ministry of Education Statistics section.

Mueller, Josef. (1990). Literacy-Human Right, Not Privilege. *D + C Development and Cooperation:* Brelin: German Foundation for International Development, No. 2:17.

Obura, A.P.. (1991). *Changing Images, Portrayal of Girls and Women in Kenyan Textbooks.* Nairobi: Acts Press.

Obura and Rogers. (1993). *Girls in Secondary Education and Women and Development in Kenya.* Nairobi. Report of a Joint Consultancy undertaken by ODA.

Republic of Kenya. (1989). *Population Census.* Nairobi: Government Printer.

Republic of Kenya. (2007). Literacy Rates. http://www.hmnet.com/africa/kenya/kenya.html

----------. (1988). *Report on Presidential Working Party on Education and Manpower Training for the next Decade and Beyond.* Nairobi: Government Printer.

----------. (1993). *Economic Survey.* Nairobi: Government Printer.

----------. (1994). *Economic Survey.* Nairobi: Government Printer.

----------. (1995). *Economic Survey.* Nairobi: Government Printer.

----------. (1996). *Economic Survey.* Nairobi: Government Printer.

----------. (1997). *Economic Survey.* Nairobi: Government Printer

----------. (2003). *Economic Survey.* Nairobi: Government Printer.

----------. (1997). *Development Plan 1997 - 2001.* Nairobi: Government Printer

Sadker, Myra Pollack, and Sadker D. Miller. (1985). "Sexism in the Schoolroom of the 80's" *Psychology Today,* March, P.55.

Sebstad J. (1992). *Gender and Employment in Kenya: Analysis of the 1988 Rural and the 1986 Urban Labour Force* Survey. (Ministry of Planning and National Development, Long Range Planning Project).

Waihenya, Kariuki. (2001). *Poor showing by Girls in Exams, Daily Nation.* Nairobi Nation Media Group.

Waithaka, M. J. (1992). *National Conference on Education for All (EFA) Kenya. Draft Report* Kisumu: Kenya.

Weekly Review. (1995). The Cabinet. A first for Kenyan Women. Nairobi: *Weekly Review Ltd*, May 12th.

Wichterich Christa. (1985). Development with 'other' Sex, A postscript on the Women's Forum in Nairobi. *D + C Development and Cooperation.* Berlin: German Foundation for International Development. No.6

11

The Teacher and the Teaching Profession

Is Teaching a Profession?

Teaching is a profession for both men and women who have undertaken a teacher education programme for the purposes of instructing pupils and students within the school system. A teacher education course is expected to equip individuals with knowledge in their subject area of specialisation as well as appropriate skills pertaining to their mode of instruction. On completion of the teacher education programme, teachers are expected to instruct, manage the learning process and guide students into becoming responsible members of the society. Scheffler (1973) characterised teaching as an activity aimed at the achievement of learning, and which is practised in such a manner as to respect students, intellectual integrity and judgement. This characterisation brings out the fact that teaching is goal-oriented, intentional and is expected to involve the learners in the learning process.

It has been noted that teaching is the largest and probably the most important profession in the world. About two-thirds of the world's population are at one time in direct contact with a teacher. In Kenya, for example, two thirds of salaried employees are either teachers or have a relative, a friend, an acquaintance or a neighbour who is a teacher (GOK/UNESCO, 1993: vii).

The teaching activities of the teacher have by far the greatest importance in the school organization. These activities are viewed as socializing actions because the teacher is employed to interact with a less socially prepared section of the society, that is, the pupils or students. Teaching activities are socially purposeful as they follow certain socially prescribed routines and methods with the aim of fulfilling a particular purpose in society.

Thus, in any educational system, the teacher and the teaching activities are two important elements that need to be given special care. It is because of such activities that the teacher and teaching activities have become an integral part of Sociology of Education. To respond effectively on whether teaching is a profession; we must explain examine features or characteristics associated with a profession and the extent to which they are met in the teaching profession in Kenya.

Characteristics of a Profession

(i) Specialized expert body of knowledge

This kind of knowledge is recognized as complex, unique and only understood by those with special knowledge in that particular field, which is only possessed by fully trained members of the profession. Examples of such professions are law, medicine, and engineering, among others.

(ii) Power and Autonomy

The reference here is with independence on the part of practitioners to make critical decisions about their profession. For instance, doctors control the conditions and contents of their own training and licensing. Teaching falls short in this aspect of power and autonomy in that teachers are often subject to rules, regulations, terms, and conditions of service decided even by non-teachers. Many Government bureaucrats and politicians who exercise authority over teachers are not trained teachers. They do not therefore sympathize with the plight of teachers. There should be regulatory body recognized by law which empowers the body to examine, admit, discipline or suspend its members into and from practising.

(iii) Commitment to a Job

Commitment should be viewed as a way of life and not just another job. Many teachers have very low commitment to teaching as a career. This is attributed to the low remunerations they receive that make them lack the incentive to be committed to their career. Teaching is characterized by long hours and low pay (Bell & Stub, 1968:269). Teachers in Kenya are said to be among the most poorly paid in East and Central Africa states (World Bank Report, 1984). In October 1998, teachers of all public schools in Kenya went on strike over remuneration package (Daily Nation, 5th October, 1998). This strike lasted for more than two weeks.

Due to low salaries and poor working conditions, teaching is usually seen as a stepping stone to other better jobs or careers, or simply a means of financing studies for higher level and better-paid careers where possible. Commitment, however, calls for dedication. A teacher who is committed will prepare for the class lessons adequately and be punctual. Due to lack of life-long commitment, many teachers rarely make the effort to be innovative in teaching of their subjects (GOK/UNESCO, 1993:40).

(iv) Profession and Social Prestige

Members of a particular profession have to be seen by the public as enjoying prestige and high social status. This implies that the term profession is an evaluative term; thus it describes and compares various careers. However, the teaching profession worldwide, and particularly in developing countries does not enjoy a lot of social prestige due to a number of factors:

- Untrained teachers are engaged in teaching. Teaching therefore does not appear to be as specialized as that of doctors and lawyers. One cannot practise as a doctor or lawyer unless trained and licensed by their respective regulatory bodies.
- Teaching in Kenya and elsewhere in the world is a low paying profession. Consequently, it attracts people of low academic ability. Such individuals make teaching be associated with mediocrity and less prestige.

Fundamentals of Sociology of Education

- Teaching profession admits people with different entry requirements. For instance, the majority of teachers in Kenya at pre-primary and primary levels in Kenya are non-degree holders. Teachers meant to teach in nursery or primary or secondary school level should therefore pursue a Bachelors of Education degree to give teaching prestige. Different entry requirements to institutions of teacher education and consequent differentiated grading or ranks fragments lowers the prestige of the teaching profession.
- Teaching is generally a rural-based occupation where conditions of living are poor compared to those in urban areas where there is electricity, tap water and generally good road networks. The poor conditions under which teachers work tend to lower the social status of the teaching profession.
- In many countries, teaching is predominantly occupied by women at lower levels. Most occupations that are female dominated such as nursing, secretarial work, catering and teaching tend to be associated with low prestige. This is partly because these occupations are lowly remunerated and also due to the fact that they are occupied by members of the society who have been accorded little social standing.

Teaching in Kenya seems to enjoy very little autonomy. For instance, what teachers teach, how they teach and evaluate is largely determined by bodies outside the teaching profession. Indeed teachers code of conduct and terms of service are developed by Teachers Service Commission, which is under the Ministry of Education and Human Resource Development rather than a teachers' professional body.

Teachers in Kenya have a Trade Union Body (Kenya National Union of Teachers) rather than a professional body. It agitates for better terms of employment, but has so far not experienced a lot of success, for it is heavily censored by the government. *The Daily Nation,* (September 11, 1993) suggested that if teachers in Kenya hoped to enhance the prestige of the teaching profession, they should establish a professional society in order to protect, safeguard and promote their professional interests. A teachers' professional body would handle the technical and professional areas of education, such as the aims of education, changes, formulation and implementation of educational curriculum, teachers' education, rights of students and advise the government accordingly in matters of education. A teachers' professional body would also provide a forum through which teachers could give their views and ideas concerning their profession, national issues, democracy and human rights.

Why do People Choose Teaching as a Career?

In spite of the fact that teaching is perceived as a low status occupation, it continues to attract many applicants. We now examine this phenomenon.

To begin with, there is an influx of teachers from the lower middle socio-economic groups of the population. To them, teaching means advancement in social status. In the case of women, it is one of the traditional occupations. This is attributed to the fact that women are said to possess certain personality traits that go well with teaching (Bell & Stub, 1968:280). Another reason why some people opt for teaching is that in spite of the long period of teacher training, the period is still shorter in comparison with other professions such as medicine or law. This aspect in itself may encourage some people to choose teaching as a career.

Sociologically, it has been shown that people who make good teachers are those of good social behaviour and introverts by nature. These people have high persistence, high emotional self-control, firm acceptance of reality, high capacity for deferred gratification, high frustration tolerance, and capacity for empathy. They are also humble. It is further shown that a higher than average ego strength may be required to grapple with the requirements of teaching (Ansu Datta, 1984:124).

Apart from sociological factors, academic requirements are also vital. Prior to the introduction of the 8-4-4 system of Education in Kenya in 1985, the minimum qualification required at the secondary school level was, and still is, O'level education for Secondary School Teacher 1 (S1) or Diploma certificate. Diploma graduates enter teacher education institutions after secondary level of education. The diploma course takes two years. The training of *S1* teachers has been replaced with the training of diploma teachers at diploma teachers training colleges at Kagumo, Kisii and Kenya Science Teachers' College, and the training of Technical teachers at the Kenya Technical Teachers College under the Ministry of Technical Training and Applied Technology. A teacher educator of a teacher training college must be a University graduate with a Bachelor of Education degree with at least two years of teaching experience at the secondary school level. University graduates with a Bachelor of Arts or Bachelor of Science degree, with a post-graduate diploma in education, are also posted to teach at teacher institutions once they acquire the necessary teaching experience at the secondary school level (GOK/UNESCO).

Categories of Teachers in Kenya's School System

The education system in Kenya has witnessed a phenomenal growth and expansion during the period after independence in 1963. Over the years since 1963, various categories of qualified and under qualified teachers have been recruited for various levels within Kenya's education system.

Primary School Level: Those who completed primary school education and possess either a Certificate of Primary Education (CPE) or the Kenya Certificate of Primary Education (KCPE) or those with secondary school education.

Secondary School Level: Those with East Africa Advanced Certificate of Education (EAACE) or Kenya Advanced Certificate of Education (KACE) with one Principal pass and 2 subsidiary passes; those with East Africa Certificate of Education (EACE) or Kenya Advanced Certificate of Education (KACE) Division III and above; trained P1 teachers with EAACE/KACE pass in Kiswahili or Islamic Religious Education (IRE); untrained technical teachers with at least EACE/KCE Division III with two years pre-service technical training in their areas of specialization - for example, woodwork, metalwork; others are trained P1 teachers with at least Grade 6 from the London

School of Music; and untrained graduate teachers with a Bachelor of Arts or Bachelor of Science degree.

Teacher Education Level: Majority of the teachers in teacher education institutions are trained and professionally qualified graduate teachers. A number of S1/diploma teachers and technical teachers with special subject knowledge such as Music, Art, Physical Education, Agriculture, Industrial Education, are posted to teach in these institutions because of their specialized skills (GOK/UNESCO, 1993:40).

Untrained teachers are those recruited to teach in primary and secondary schools and have not been professionally trained through in-service or pre-service programmes. On the other hand, under qualified teachers are those who may be trained or untrained, but are posted to teach at levels for which they are not qualified. Majority of teachers in primary and secondary school are trained. Unfortunately, 54.5% of teachers in pre-primary schools are untrained.

Why most People do not Choose Teaching as a Career

A number of factors discourage people from training as a teacher. Foremost, the attitudes of families and friends influences in varying degree especially if the aspirant is a male. The neutral attitude toward the girl who intends to teach may acquire an acid tone if she wants to teach in the elementary school. A liberal arts student will consider elementary school teaching as an acceptable female occupation but as an undesirable way of living for a man (Bell and Stub, 1968:282). There is correlation between the status in which students of liberal arts colleges hold teaching and their rating of the contribution the teacher makes to society. In terms of social prestige, a secondary teacher may rank at the bottom of twelve occupations (such as medicine, engineering, law), on a par with salesmen and small-business proprietors, even though above elementary school teachers. As a contributor to society, he rises to the fourth rank from the top, above lawyers, engineers and business executives, and below medical doctors.

Though a good number of young people train as teachers, they quit the teaching profession either immediately after completion of training or soon after employment. Each year, many thousands leave the profession due to a number of reasons: Firstly, teachers work for long hours and in addition, pupils are too many for the teachers to handle effectively in terms of giving each pupil proper attention. Secondly, clerical routines and community projects tend to distract them from professional purpose; they leave them with little time to devote to education and professional matters. Thirdly, salaries are inadequate, facilities, e.g. buildings and equipment, are unsatisfactory (GOK/UNESCO, 1993:35). Due to these reasons, many trained teachers are not retained in the profession. Those who remain engage in other activities to generate additional income that supplements their salary at the expense of their duty.

The Changing Multiple Roles of the Teacher

The structural context of the school presents the incumbent teacher's role with the task of continuous integration and adjustment of conflicting expectations. A teacher's role varies depending on our view of the arena in which the teacher operates. Thus, there is a significant range of adaptation among teachers in their capacity to harmonize the conflicting tendencies in their roles. The teacher operates both within the school perimeters and the wider community as well. A teacher's role is therefore diversified.

The Roles of the Teacher within the School

In many ways, the teacher's status in the school can be compared to that of a foreman in a factory. Like the foreman, the teacher is the "person in the middle", subject to conflicting social demands from above and below. Both teacher and foreman are key functionaries in implementing organizational goals. The two occupational roles require the utilization of considerable social skills in interpersonal relations in order to gain close cooperation on one hand, and to maintain the status of expertness and authority on the other. The teacher and the foreman both lack the unambiguous status necessary for maintaining a consistent degree of autonomy; yet both roles demand a measure of independence in order to be effectively fulfilled (Bell and Stub, 1968:259).

Within the school, the teacher has a number of sub-roles. In the first place, the teacher has to relate to other adults in various capacities. In relation to fellow teachers and employer, he or she must play the role of an employee. To the subordinate staff, he or she is their boss. Of interest, however, is the role of the teacher in relation to pupils:

(i) Mediator of learning

In this role, the teacher transmits knowledge and directs the learning process. This is perhaps the most important of all the teacher's roles. The majority of teachers are usually thoroughly prepared to perform this role through professional training. This involves mastery of subject matter and methodology of delivery, all of which are taught during one's training. The criterion for gauging success in this area is by testing and grading. The teacher's success is measured in terms of pupil's progress through school.

(ii) The teacher as a disciplinarian

This role requires that the teacher be in command of the classroom situation in order to optimize the learning process. This role is often a source of conflict for most teachers. This is because a teacher has to make careful observations of a child's developing abilities and skills, provide the appropriate experiences just at the right time, be on hand with exciting and worthwhile experiences when the time is ripe, provide opportunities for self-esteem and the utilization of unique abilities. She/he also has to encourage the child's creativity at every turn, help the child to discover and understand him/herself as a person, understand the defence mechanisms of anxious children who without such understanding may become poor learners, aggressive, and antisocial citizens. He/she has to create a desire for learning and an eagerness for life in the minds of the students because the teacher feels that way about learning and life.

Teachers who are relatively new to the profession normally find it difficult to handle problems associated with discipline in schools. They do not know whether to be strict or lenient.

(iii) The teacher as a judge of students' performance

In academic matters, a teacher has authority to grade students and to promote them to the next class or level of learning. Apart from academics, the teacher also decides what is wrong or right behaviour in other areas of interaction. In judging, the teacher either rewards acceptable behaviour with material or and verbal means, or punishes a student for wrong behaviour. For example, well-behaved students are given books, pens, and trophies of appreciation. They may also get certificates of recognition for their behaviour. On the other hand, misconduct is reprimanded and if it a serious case such as involvement in drug taking, destruction of property, stealing and fighting with other students, they are expelled from school.

(iv) The teacher as a confidant

The role of a teacher as a friend or confidant is very vital. This is because the teacher is seen as a supportive adult in whom children can place trust and affection. Thus, it is mandatory that the teacher develops friendship with the pupils in order to open up communication channels.

(v) The teacher as surrogate parent

This role of the teacher is very important especially in lower classes. Here, the teacher has to comfort, praise or scold the pupil accordingly. The teacher also has to assist the pupil with certain basic tasks such as dressing, tying shoe laces etc. Besides the role of a surrogate parent, the teacher acts as a counsellor during and after school hours. A good rapport between the teacher and the pupils is vital for them to appreciate this surrogate role of the teacher. This rapport will assist the pupils/students to develop confidence in the teacher.

(vi) The teacher as the carrier of the middle class values

Community members, especially the rural people, regard teaching as a senior profession. Thus, the teacher is expected to live the life of a middle class professional. The teacher is supposed to exemplify the attributes of the middle class, that is, good morals, dependability and good citizenship.

Teacher's Role within the Community

Within the wider community, the teacher has a number of sub-roles to fulfil. Firstly, is the expectation that the teacher should be an active participant in community affairs. In the rural areas, there is the demand for the teacher to engage in community activities such as welfare organizations, and religious functions among others. Hence, in addition to the professional duties which the teacher is required to execute, the community also looks upon the teacher to provide expert advice in the running of community's activities.

Secondly, the teacher plays the role of a public servant. This service is concerned with the intellectual and moral development of children and youths. In other words, the teacher is expected to be exemplary in behaviour and morals as an example to the young to imitate. A teacher, therefore, is expected not to be a drunkard, a smoker or to be careless in dressing and grooming. The teacher also should not engage in immoral activities.

Thirdly, the community views the teacher as the doyen of the middle class. The community, in other words, expects the teacher to use correct speech, have good manners, be modest and prudent, honest, and be responsible and friendly. Generally, the rural community expects a teacher to live a more comfortable life than them because of the social status they ascribe to the teaching profession.

In summary, one can say that the roles of the teacher are very diffuse. They embrace wide latitude of activities and expectations. The teacher is concerned with the total development of the individual child in the classroom and school as a whole. This includes the child's intellectual, spiritual, moral and physical growth. The teacher is charged with the responsibility of moulding morally upright, socially adjusted and productive members of the society.

Conflict in Social Roles of the Teacher

Conflict in the social roles of a teacher originates from three areas. The first is the socio-economic role. Teachers are expected by the public to maintain high standards of living and life styles that may be beyond their reach. This is quite a big problem that put teachers in a dilemma. As a result, therefore, many teachers leave the profession, and those who remain resort to other activities to supplement their meagre salaries.

The second area of conflict is the citizen role of the teacher. Though teachers are expected to participate in certain public activities such as religious and welfare activities of the community, their participation in local politics is somehow curtailed. This is very much the case especially in Africa. The fact that teachers cannot really participate in political affairs tends to limit their freedom of citizenry to a certain extent (Ansu Datta, 1984:121).

The third area of conflict for the teacher is the role of an expert. The teacher, like any other professional, specializes in a particular academic field or subject(s). However, the teacher often finds himself or herself in a situation where the curricula and syllabi expects him or her to handle a subject that is outside his or her knowledge. This puts the teacher in a dilemma and in a challenging situation.

Despite the teacher facing some of these conflicting demands, it is important to remember that teachers are not different from other professionals. Their problems are not necessarily unique to them. Other professionals experience similar problems and difficulties, or perhaps even more serious. The most important thing is to learn how to cope with the situation without breaking down.

Perception of the Teacher by the Students

In examining the perceptions of the teacher's role, the feelings and views of pupils should not be ignored. The way pupils rate teachers differs between industrialized and less industrialized countries. For the industrialized countries, research has shown that pupils value most the intellectual competence and teaching effectiveness of the teacher. The teacher's personality, scalability and managerial skills are least valued. Pupils expect teachers to teach; they value lucid exposition, the clear statement of problems, and guidance in their solutions. Personal qualities of kindness, sympathy and patience are secondary. They are appreciated by pupils only if they make the teacher more effective in carrying out his or her primary intellectual task (Musgrave and Taylor, 1965).

The ratings of teachers by African students are different. These students prefer teachers who know their subjects well but who at the same time show an understanding of students' problems. In other words, the good teacher is both intelligent, proficient as a teacher and cooperatively the class. The teacher with a sense of duty and vocation is also highly appreciated (Olatunde and Ade Ademola, 1985). But the ratings of a bad teacher are not very different from students in both industrialized and less industrialized countries. A bad teacher is one who knows little about his or her subject, one who teaches poorly, one who is arrogant and does not show empathy, uncooperative even if intelligent, a sadist and oppressive. A teacher who is a tyrant may be feared but is rarely appreciated or held up as a role model of the good teacher (Ansu Datta, 1984:122). Since society is dynamic and social changes are experienced in all facets of life, the role(s) of the teacher also change from the perspectives of the parents, the pupils and the community at large.

Summary

The profession of teaching had a very humble beginning. It actually originated with the missionaries or Christendom. Although a humble profession, it is a noble profession since all other professionals pass through the hands of a teacher. In spite of the teachers' hard work, they are poorly remunerated. As a result therefore, many trained, teachers leave the profession for greener pastures. Those who are retained, engage in other activities to generate additional income.

Teachers often find themselves in a conflict because of the many different roles they are expected to play. Sometimes the societal demands on the teacher are what make the situation worse. The way the society expects the teacher to live and conduct him/herself is beyond the teacher's means of sustenance. Students from industrialized and less industrialized countries rate teachers differently; there is somehow a general consensus. All agree that a good teacher is one who has good command of his or her subject matter, cooperative and morally upright.

Study Questions

1. In the recent past in Kenya, teachers have been going on strike over poor remuneration package. In your view, describe what can be done so as to improve the teaching profession and also attract more qualified people to join it.

2. As a potential teacher in contemporary Kenya, what changes are you experiencing regarding your role(s)?

3. Make a visit to a school and find out from students the qualities they associate with a good teacher.

References

Ansu, Datta. (1984). *Education and Society: A Sociology of African Education.* London: MacMillan Publishers.

Bell, R., and Stub, H.R. (1968). *The Sociology of Education.* Illinois: The Dorsey Press.

Daily Nation Newspapers Ltd. (1998). *Daily Nation* 5th October and 23rd October. Nairobi: Nation Group of Newspapers Limited.

GOK/UNESCO. (1993). *Status of Teachers in Kenya: A National Case Study.* Nairobi: Kenya Education Staff Institute.

Musgrave, and Taylor, Olatunde, O. and Ade Ademola. (1985). *Sociology: An Introductory African Text.* London: MacMillan Publishers.

Republic of Kenya. (2001). *Economic Survey.* Nairobi: Government Printer.

Scheffler, I. (1973). *Reason and Teaching* . London: Routledge and Kegan Paul

Sifuna, D.N. and Otiende, J. E.. (1994). *An Introductory History of Education.* Nairobi: Nairobi University Press.

World Bank. (1984). *World Bank Report.* NewYork: World Bank.

12

Who Joins the Teaching Profession?
A Case Study of Undergraduate Students' Attitudes and Perceptions Towards the Teaching Profession

Introduction

This chapter is based on findings of a study of undergraduate students' attitudes and perceptions towards the teaching profession.[1] The participating students had already completed all teacher education courses including practical teaching when this investigation was carried out. The results of this study revealed that a large proportion of students (56%) did not choose teaching as their first choice career. These students had preferred to join either Medicine or Commerce or Engineering or Law. However, they did not perform well enough at Kenya Certificate of Secondary Education (KCSE) to merit admission to such competitive fields.

The majority of the participants did not intend to remain in the teaching profession. Some 10.2% of them said they would look for alternative employment on graduation while 57% would take up teaching while waiting to secure non-teaching jobs. Another finding of this study is that a large proportion of individuals from rural and low social economic backgrounds join the teaching profession. This

---

[1] *First published in* **Kenya Journal of Education** *by Kariuki and Kibera. Vol 6, 1996 under "University Students' Attitudes ad Perceptions Toward the teaching Profession and teaching practice".*

is consistent with earlier findings on the topic (Foster, 1965; Clignet and Foster, 1966; Chivore, 1986; and Achola, 1987).

What is Teacher Education?

Teacher education refers to professional education and training of teachers. It consists of course work in academic and professional subjects combined with supervised practice teaching. Basically, teacher education gives student teachers opportunities to acquire academic knowledge in either Science or Arts or Technical Subjects. The academic subjects studied by the student teacher, become their teaching subjects in schools once teacher education course is completed whereas the professional component of teacher education which in Kenya comprise education courses such as Philosophy of Education, History of Education, Sociology of Education, Educational Psychology, General Methods of Teaching, Subject Methods, Educational Planning, Educational Administration, Curriculum Development and Practical Teaching. These subjects are expected to equip student teachers with theoretical framework guiding education and the necessary pedagogical skills.

In essence, therefore, teacher education combines academic, professional subjects and training. Training constitutes practical teaching. This exercise initiates and guides student teachers in the application of teaching and classroom management techniques in actual classroom learning situations. Combination of theoretical education courses with practical training is crucial in the education of teachers. This is because possession of academic knowledge is not adequate if one does not know how to pass it on to pupils.

On the other hand, training is not enough if the individual has no knowledge and the rationale to pass it on. Education and training makes teacher education complete. In spite of the right combination of education for teachers, there are several issues that require attention in order to enhance their full and effective participation in the teaching profession. First, it is important to find out whether the individuals who join teacher education programme are genuinely interested in the teaching profession or merely join it because opportunities to enter other professions do not exist. If it turns out that the majority of those in the teaching profession had not initially intended to be teachers, it can be argued that such individuals did not exercise their democratic right to pursue careers of their choice. Existence of such a scenario may lead us to conclude that the majority of individuals in the teaching profession lack enthusiasm, interest and motivation to teach despite undergoing teacher education programme.

The major objective of the study was to establish the characteristics of individuals admitted to faculties of education and their attitudes and perceptions towards the teaching profession. To get an insight into this issue, literature on peoples' attitudes and perceptions towards the teaching profession was reviewed. Additionally, the questionnaire solicited information from student teachers about their views of the teaching profession.

Characteristics of Individuals who Join the Teaching Profession

A number of studies on people's attitudes and perceptions towards the teaching profession have shown that the teaching profession is popular among individuals from a rural background as well as those from the low socio-economic status. Some of the early studies by Foster (1965), Clignet and Foster (1966), Chivore (1986) and Achola (1987) have confirmed this position. The explanation for this phenomenon has been attributed to the predominance of the teaching career in the rural areas. Teachers in the rural schools act as models for many of their students in their occupational choices. Besides, teaching compared to other jobs that are available in the rural areas such as peasant farming, petty trading or working as farm labourers, is a much more prestigious and a better remunerated occupation. Teaching, therefore, seems to be regarded by rural communities as the first step in the process of upward mobility.

This case study sought to find out whether teaching continues to attract individuals from rural communities vis-à-vis those from urban areas. This is in recognition of the fact that urban-based employment in the less industrialised countries have been on the decline. The teaching force has, however, been growing steadily in order to cope with the increased student population in schools. Increase in student population in schools has resulted from the high birth rate and the fact that today, many more children survive due to improved medical care. It is quite possible then, that individuals from urban areas have found solace in the teaching profession in the belief that they are more likely to be assured of jobs.

This study has also attempted to find out other factors that attract people to join the teaching profession. Researchers who have studied decision making in occupational choice have argued that occupational choice is determined by a multiplicity of factors. Hicks (1966) found out the factors that make a job prestigious include, money earned, responsibility attached to the job, intelligence and education needed to do the job, service rendered to others while doing the job, power and influence gained while discharging the job. From this study, he concluded that these characteristics influence career choices in varying degrees.

Holland (1959) also observed that occupational choice was a matter of attempting to maximise personality characteristics and occupational attributes. Thus, decision-making in occupational choice is a complex issue and it is influenced by a myriad of factors such as availability of job opportunities, income and fringe benefits attached to a particular job, working conditions and personality characteristics such as ability and interest to do a job. Herzberg (1964) developed the idea that there are two sets of conditions that affected a person at work. He called one set motivators and the other hygiene factors. The first set of motivators included achievement, recognition, work itself, responsibility and advancement or growth because of the nature of the task. This set of factors is said to be intrinsic to the job. According to Herzberg, if these factors are not present in a job, the worker will not necessarily be dissatisfied, but the individual will not be highly motivated. Reduced motivation is likely to lead to low job output.

The hygiene factors include, things like company policies, administrative procedures, supervision, interpersonal relations, salary and working conditions. These hygiene factors are rather external or extrinsic to the job. According to Herzberg these factors do not tend to be motivators. They only keep workers from becoming dissatisfied. Herzberg's theory is relevant to this study, in the sense that it will help us to discover what factors student teachers attach to the teaching profession and from these we can deduce their consequent effects in their performance as teachers in Kenyan Secondary Schools. The theory may also help us to answer questions such as:

- Why do some individuals choose teaching as a profession while others do not?
- Is it possible that individuals drift into Teacher Education as a result of their failure to be admitted to programmes of their choice?
- If so, does the teacher education programme which they undergo make them aspire to be teachers?

Presentation of Findings

The sample surveyed was in their second year of study from the Faculty of Education, University of Nairobi. They comprised 138 student teachers, 87 males (63%) and 51 were females (37%). Their age ranged between 20-29 years. However, the majority of student teachers (65.3%) were between 20 and 22 years of age.

The students recruited to the teacher education programme were among those who had met the minimum university admission criterion at the end of their secondary education. The secondary schools from which these students came are located in seven out of eight provinces of the Republic of Kenya. These included Nairobi, Coast, Nyanza, Rift Valley, Eastern, Western and Central provinces. There were none from North Eastern province. This province has lagged behind in education. It is mainly inhabited by nomadic peoples whose large numbers have not yet embraced school education due to socio-economic and cultural factors.

With regards to the student teachers' socio-economic status as indicated by the level of their fathers', education mothers' education, and occupations, it turned out that the majority of students came from the low Socio-Economic Status (SES). In this study, parents with no education and primary education were placed in the low SES and they were the majority, while those with secondary education were placed in the middle Socio-Economic Status. Parents with post secondary education and university degrees were placed in the high SES.

With respect to occupation, parents holding unskilled and manual semi-skilled jobs were placed in the low SES while parents occupying artisan and clerical service related jobs were placed in the middle SES. Finally, parents occupying administrative and professional occupations were designated high SES. Tables 1 and 2 carry information on the educational level of the student teachers' fathers and mothers.

Table 1: Fathers' level of Education

Level of Education	Frequency	Per cent (%)
None	24	18.3
Primary	29	22.1
Secondary	43	32.8
Post Secondary Diploma	20	15.3
University	15	11.5
Total	**131**	**100%**

From this analysis, it is evident that only 15.3% of the student teachers had fathers with post secondary diploma qualifications; 11.5% with university degrees and 32.8% with secondary education. Some 18.3% of the parents had no formal education while 22.1% had primary education.

With respect to their mothers' level of education, only 11.3% of the student teachers had mothers with post secondary Diploma qualification and above. Table 2 carries the pertinent data.

Table 2: Mothers' level of education

Level of Education	Frequency	Per cent (%)
None	31	25.0
Primary	43	34.7
Secondary	36	29.0
Post Secondary Diploma	12	9.7
University	2	1.6
Total	**124**	**100%**

With regards to fathers' and mothers' occupation, the data elicited indicated that 3% of the fathers were farmers, 15.1% teachers and 41.6% professionals. The rest 41.3% were unemployed or worked as petty traders or drivers or artisans. With respect to mothers' occupation, 37.6% of the mothers were farmers and 16% teachers. Some were 2.2% nurses, 1.4% secretaries, 0.7% lawyers, 0.2% artisans and 25.6% were petty traders. The rest (69.9%) were unemployed. This means that the mothers were housewives as it is difficult to imagine an "unemployed" mother in the actual sense of the term.

The data in tables 1 and 2 confirm that the teaching profession still remains a popular occupation among individuals from the low socio-economic status as measured by the parental level of education and the type of occupation they hold. After discussing the socio-economic status of teacher education students, information on the location of their parents' residences was analysed. The results are presented in Table 3.

The results indicate that teaching continues to be popular among students from rural communities. An overwhelming majority (87.7%) of the parents of student teachers resided in the rural areas. In addition, the distribution of student teachers by province confirms that Nairobi Province, which is also the capital city, had very few students who had joined the teacher education programme.

Table 3: Students teachers' area of residence

Type of Residence	Frequency	Percent
Rural	121	87.7
Urban	17	12.3
Total	**138**	**100%**

Coast Province, which has also the second largest city in Kenya (Mombasa), was in a similar situation as shown on Table 4.

Table 4: Student teachers by province of Kenya

Provinces	Frequency	Percent
Central	31	22.5
Nairobi	3	2.2
Western	17	12.3
Nyanza	28	20.3
Rift Valley	33	23.7
Eastern	22	15.9
Coast	4	2.9
Total	**138**	**100%**

These results reveal that Nairobi and Coast provinces had very few student teachers possibly because of the urban nature of these two provinces where alternative career choices exist. The analysis of the student teachers' socio-economic status and their places of residence reveal that the teaching profession continues to be popular among individuals from low SES and rural backgrounds.

Next, we discuss data on student – teachers' attitudes and perception towards the teaching profession.

Student teachers' attitudes and perceptions of the teaching profession

The student teachers' attitudes and perceptions were tested by examining the number of students who had applied for the teaching profession as their first choice vis-à-vis those who had not but were "forced" by circumstances to take it up. The pertinent results are contained in tables 5 and 6. The data in Table 5 shows that 55.5% of student teachers had not preferred teaching as their first choice career. Thus, only 44.5% opted to join teaching as their most preferred career.

Table 5: Was teaching your first choice career?

Responses	Frequency	Percent
Yes	61	44.5
No	76	55.5
Total	**137**	**100%**

The reasons why some students chose teaching as their career are presented in Table 6 below.

Table 6: Students teachers' reasons for choosing teaching as their first choice career

Reasons	Frequency	Percent
Social career	8	12.5
Satisfying job	19	29.7
Like sharing knowledge	4	6.3
Enables one to live in rural area	3	4.7
Required low admission points	4	6.3
Job security	12	18.3
Enables one to work anywhere in the country	14	21.9
Total	**64**	**100%**

Fundamentals of Sociology of Education

The results in table 6 suggest that the majority of student teachers chose teaching as their first choice career mainly on the basis of job attributes external to the teaching profession. Such job attributes included: teaching is a "sociable career," "there is job security," and "teaching opportunities are available all over the country."

The analysis has also revealed that over 6.3% of the student teachers perceived teaching as an occupation which is not competitive and therefore could admit individuals with low abilities. We also notice also that only about 29% of the students-teachers indicated that teaching was a satisfying job. We may therefore conclude that the majority of individuals who end up in the teaching profession do not find it satisfying, a condition that may lead to low interest and lack of self-drive to perform well in the teaching profession. The career may only be a stepping-stone to other more challenging, satisfying and financially rewarding occupations. The individuals who did not indicate teaching as their first choice occupation but were "drafted" into the teaching profession cited reasons analyzed in Table 7 for not having chosen it.

Table 7: Student teachers' reasons for making teaching a first choice career

Reasons	Frequency	Percent
Low pay/promotion opportunities are rare.	24	35.8
Lack of interest	29	43.2
Public criticism	4	6.0
Teaching is regarded a low profession	5	7.5
Total	**62**	**100%**

The results in table 7 indicate that (43.2%) of the student teachers who had not selected teaching but found themselves in the teaching faculty, had cited lack of interest as the principal reason for not opting to enter the teaching profession. It appears then that the teaching profession is practised by individuals who have no motivation or natural aptitude for the job. They simply take it on in order to earn a living. The majority of the students who had not selected teaching as their first choice had hoped to join other more "prestigious" occupations as shown in Table 8.

Table 8: First choice career by student teachers "forced" into teaching

Professions	Frequency	Percent
Law	40	60.6
Commerce	18	27.3
Medicine	2	3.0
Bachelor of Arts	5	7.6
Hotel Management	1	1.5
Total	**66**	**100%**

The results in table 8 reveal that among the students who found themselves in teacher education but had not indicated it as a first choice included (60.6%) who wanted to do law, (27.3%) Commerce, (6.6%), Bachelor of Arts, (3%) Medicine, (7.6%) and 1.5% Hotel Management.

Further insights into the reasons and circumstances that led students to join the teaching profession are presented in table 9.

From this analysis, it is evident that 42.4% of the student teachers "drifted" into the teaching profession for lack of adequate alternative occupational opportunities. However, 32.1% of the student teachers had made a decision to join the teaching profession on their own volition. The rest (11.7%) said they had been influenced by fathers, 2.2%) mothers. (8.0%) teachers and by older siblings (3.6%).

It is clear then that, only 32.1% of the students in the sample selected teaching as their career and profession on their own " free-will".

Table 9: People and circumstances that influenced students to enter the teaching profession

People	Frequency	Percent
Self	44	32.1
Father	16	11.7
Mother	3	2.2
Teachers	11	8.0
Older siblings	5	3.6
Lack of adequate alternative occupations	58	42.4
Total	**137**	**100%**

The question then arises: Is the teacher education programme rigorous enough to convince the "draftees" into the teaching profession to make teaching their career? Table 10 presents data on student teachers' career plans after obtaining the bachelor of education degree.

Table 10: Student teachers' career intentions/plans after obtaining the bachelor of education degree

Career Intentions	Frequency	Percent
Join Teaching Profession	45	32.8
Seek Non-teaching Job	14	10.2
Take Up-Teaching while looking for another job	78	57.0
Total	**137**	**100%**

The results in table 10 seem to indicate that the teacher education programme does not transform individuals who had not initially chosen teaching into wanting to be teachers. For instance, 10.2% of such individuals would seek for non-teaching occupations on graduation while 57% would take up teaching until they secured a non-teaching occupation.

In conclusion, it is clear that the teaching profession continues to be popular among individuals from low SES and with a rural background. The analysis has also revealed that the majority of individuals who undertake teacher education programme do so because of their failure to secure admission into their first choice career programmes like law, medicine and commerce. Indeed, their lack of motivation for the teaching profession persisted in spite of their acknowledgement that teacher education programme was relevant and useful in the education of teachers. Clearly then, teacher education programme did not seem to convince students who did not initially choose teaching as their first choice career, to become teachers.

The findings again reveal that a good proportion of individuals in the teacher education programme cited job security, personal relationships, and working environment as the factors that made them choose teaching as their career rather than attributes such as interest and ability to do the job, which according to Herzberg (1964), are attributes intrinsic to the job and are associated with high motivation and output. Thus, it is reasonable to assume that teachers who lack interest in the teaching profession are likely not to perform as well as they should because they lack motivation and commitment to the profession. Given that teaching is often a "forced" choice career for the majority of individuals, it is worthwhile to explore the status of the teaching profession.

The Status of the Teaching Profession in Kenya

Teaching is the work or the profession of teachers. Broadly speaking, teachers educate pupils in schools up to the secondary level. According to Page (1977), the term profession is an evaluative term describing the occupation while the term status refers to the perceived social prestige or social ranking a profession enjoys in comparison with other professions.

Historically, teaching has been viewed as a low status occupation. One of the contributing factors to the low status of the teaching profession particularly in less industrialised countries like Kenya is that it sometimes engages untrained teachers. According to Ezewu (1986) members of a particular profession have to be specially prepared for the jobs they perform by a prolonged course of training. Professions are founded on systematic knowledge that requires a lengthy period and practical training. Engagement of untrained teachers in the school system depreciates the status of the teaching profession. This practice seems to strongly suggest that teaching does not require any special talents and training and therefore, almost anyone can teach. The situation at pre-primary school level is bad because 54.5% of teachers are untrained (Republic of Kenya, 2001). In addition, the teaching profession generally attracts individuals of low intellectual calibre compared to other professions. Often, it is joined by a large proportion of individuals who fail to meet high academic admission criterion for programmes such as medicine, law and engineering. Any profession that attracts mediocrity is assigned a low status.

Members of the teaching profession are not well remunerated when compared to members of other professions. Indeed, graduates entering the teaching profession in Kenya start at a salary scale lower than those in other professions such as engineers, economists, lawyers, and doctors, among others. Teachers in Kenya are likely to be among the most poorly paid in East and Central African countries (Wolff, 1984). In 1998 and 2002, teachers staged strikes to protest the poor remuneration (Mwanzia, 2002). Several Kenya Government Commissions recommended improvement in the remuneration of teachers including:

- The Republic of Kenya, Report of the Commission of Inquiry (Public Service Structure and Remuneration Commission (1971).
- Republic of Kenya, Report of the Civil Service Review Committee (1980).
- Republic of Kenya, Report of the Civil Service Committee, (1985).

In 1985, Kenyatta University Education Students demanded salary remuneration equal to those of other professions on graduation. This demand led to a temporary closure of the university.

Perhaps, the most important contributory determinant of the low status of the teaching profession in Kenya is that its members have very little autonomy. Unlike lawyers and doctors, teachers are controlled by organisations outside their own. The practice of teachers in all government schools is guided by a code of conduct prescribed by the Teachers Service Commission (TSC), which is a body under the Ministry of Education. Additionally, teachers are not in control of what they teach and how they teach it. What teachers teach and how they teach it is largely determined by other bodies. For example, Kenya Institute of Education (KIE) develops the curriculum for secondary and primary schools and also prescribes how it is to be taught. The inspectorate department of the Ministry of Education monitors the education standards while the Kenya National Examination Council (KNEC) sets examinations and organises their marking.

If they are not to be mere agents of others, for example, the state and bureaucrats teachers as specialists in the field need to set-up an autonomous agency through which a critical and continual evaluation of the purposes and the consequences of their profession are determined. Such an agency will also protect and safeguard their professional interests. Even though Kenyan teachers have a trade union body, the Kenya National Union of Teachers (KNUT), its activities are heavily monitored by the government. In addition, the organisation does not participate fully in the designing of educational policies and in determining how such policies are implemented. This organisation is also weak because its members are fragmented by their varied academic backgrounds at which they entered teacher education. Some individuals enter teacher education after primary level of education; others at secondary while others join it at university level. Lack of homogeneity in the qualifications of teachers weakens the organisational capabilities and common purpose for the members of teaching profession.

Ways of Improving the Teaching Profession

Firstly, teacher education should be a precondition for any person attaining the status of the teacher. Untrained personnel should not be permitted to teach. Involvement of such people in teaching lowers the status of the teaching profession. Additionally, such people cause untold damage on the pupils they teach; they often retard their learning since they employ inappropriate methods of teaching. In addition, they are likely to have problems in managing classroom discipline of the students because they lack the professional training.

Secondly, teaching should not be a career for those who fail to make the grade for other professions. While good academic grades may not guarantee that individuals will turn out to be good teachers, good grades may nonetheless ensure that such individuals have adequate subject content to pass on to the students. Thus, there should be a minimum entry qualification for all those entering the teaching profession. Different entry points only serve to rob the teaching profession of its prestige. Individuals who join teaching because it is a satisfying career and because they like to be knowledgeable should be identified and recruited to the teaching profession.

Thirdly, terms and conditions of teachers should be comparable to those of other professions. Improvement in terms and conditions for teachers will hopefully help to attract bright individuals who would otherwise seek careers in more lucrative fields.

Finally, members of the teaching profession should establish professional and trade union bodies. The professional body would handle the professional areas of education, such as the aims of education, pedagogy, formulation and implementation of educational curriculum, teacher education curriculum; while the trade union body would formulate or update the code of ethics for teachers, including determination of individuals who qualify to join the teaching profession. Membership of teachers to their professional and trade union bodies will give teachers the co-operative effort required for them to be able to influence policies and events particularly in the educational arena.

Study questions

1. Identify a man and a woman teacher who have resigned from the teaching profession and make an in-depth study why they quit the teaching profession.

2. Visit a college of teacher education and ask 60 girls and 60 boys why they have taken up training for teaching.

3. Looking back today, what do you think were the most important factors that made you join the teaching profession?

References

Achola, Paul, P.W., (1987). Selected Social Attitudes of Zambian Youth: Findings of National Study. Lusaka: *Educational Research Bureau*, University of Zambia.

Chivore, B.R.S., (1986). Form IV Pupils' Perceptions and Attitudes Towards the teaching Profession in Zimbabwe, *Comparative Education*. Califax Publishing Ltd pp.252-258.

Clignet and Foster, (1966). *The Fortunate Few: A Study of Secondary Schools in Ivory Coast.* Northern University Press, 1966.

Cohen, Lewis, *A Guide to Teaching Practice*, London: Methuane Ltd.

Ezewu, Edward, (1986). *Sociology of Education*. London Longman.

Foster, P., (1965). *Education and Social changes in Ghana.* London: Routledge and Kegan Paul.

Herzberg, F., (1984). *Work and the Nature of Man*. Cheveland: World.

Hicks, R.E., (1966). Occupational Prestige and its Facts. *African Social Research.* Vol. I pp. 41-58.

Holland, L.J., (1959). A Theory of Vocational Choice *Journal of CounsellingPsychology,* Vol 6 Spring pp.35-45.

Kariuki, W.P., and Kibera L.W., (1996). University Students' Attitudes and Perceptions Towards the Teaching Profession and Teaching Practice.

Mannheim, K., and Stewart, W.A.C., (1962). Kenya Journal of Education Vol 6. *An Introduction to the Sociology of Education.* Routledge.

Page, G.T., (1977). *International Dictionary of Education.* London: Niclolas Publishing Company.

Glossary

African Indigenous Education - a system of education that transmitted knowledge, skills, moral training, norms and values to the incoming generations among African societies in pre-colonial Africa.

Anomie - social chaos resulting from absence of guidelines for proper conduct of behaviour.

Authority - legitimate power.

Caste - a social category with membership ascribed or determined at birth.

Caste system - a social stratification system in which no (or almost no) mobility from one social category (caste) to another is possible.

Census - a complete count of population.

Charismatic authority - the rule based on belief in the extraordinary personal qualities of the ruler.

Church - an organisation designed to deal with the religious needs of the masses in society.

Class or (social class) - a social category with its members in the same economic situation.

Classless society - a society with no structured social mobility.

Community - a group of people occupying a territory and sharing sufficiently wide-ranging goals so that the individual's life may be lived wholly within that area.

Conflict theory - a theoretical orientation emphasizing the opposition among groups or social relationships.

Contest mobility - a pattern of educational mobility in which individual attempts to achieve elite status by means of open contests such as examinations and interviews which continue over a period of time.

Culture - culture refers to social behaviour patterns, beliefs, arts, institutions, and ways of doing things which are characteristic of a particular group of people.

Dependent variable - a variable which changes in response to changes in an independent or predictor variable.

Division of labour - specialisation among tasks organized around a central goal.

Education - a process through which a society's way of life in terms of knowledge, skills and moral values are passed on to the incoming generation.

Equality of Educational Opportunity - equality of educational opportunity is expresses a political belief encompassing an ideal educational system where all children have equal chance to develop their abilities and aptitudes to the fullest regardless of family, social class, race, and religion and gender.

Equality of opportunity - a situation in which members have equal or similar opportunities to attain positions on the higher levels of the stratification system.

Ethno-methodology - a theoretical orientation aimed at describing how people in everyday interactions construct their reality.

Evolutionary theory - a theoretical orientation emphasizing the improving adaptation of society to its environment as a mechanism of societal change.

Exchange theory - a theoretical orientation emphasizing the goals, rewards, and punishments associated with interaction.

Experiment - a procedure for collecting information through (1) actively changing a situation, such as altering an independent variable, and (2) systematically recording results obtained under two or more conditions, such as assessing changes in dependent variable.

Family - a social structure made up of people related by blood, marriage, or adoption.

Female - being of the sex that has ovaries and produces ova.

Function - a social structure's consequences for society which improve society's adaptation or adjustment.

Gender - a set of qualities and behaviours expected from a female or male by their society.

Hidden curriculum - norms, beliefs and attitudes reflected in the school practices, behaviour of teachers, students and society at large.

Hypothesis - a tentative idea or statement about how to solve a problem or about the nature or reality.

Independent variable - a variable which, as it changes, influences changes in a dependent, or criterion or response variable.

Interview schedules - guides for interviewing which include questions to be asked.

Language - a system of symbols that helps people to communicate past experiences and apply them to the present.

Learning - a relatively permanent change in behaviour that occurs as a result of experience.

Legal authority - rule based on law or formal decrees and regulations

Male - means being of sex that produces sperm.

Mores - norms generally regarded as essential for the welfare of society.

Norm - an expectation widely shared within society (or a subgroup of the society).

Observation - a procedure for collecting information by informally recording descriptions of behaviour seen or observed.

Operational definitions - procedures for measuring the phenomena to which a concept refers.

Peer groups - a group of similar age and background.

Probability sampling - a sampling procedure in which each individual or unit has a known chance/probability of being chosen.

Religion - an institution which coordinates theology or beliefs, faith, or emotional expression and ritual or actions, as solutions to the problems of ultimate significance in society.

Resource - non-material as well as material factors used to achieve goals.

Revolution - a social movement involving some degree of fundamental change.

Sampling procedures - techniques designed to achieve precise measurement.

Sexism - discrimination or prejudice against other people because of their sex.

School - a social institution set aside for deliberately educating children, pupils and students in selected aspects of knowledge, skills, and moral values that are perceived to be useful to society.

Science - an institution focusing on continuing development of knowledge based on methods which accept no assumption as sacred.

Scientific method - a process for developing knowledge based on (1) defining a problem, (2) constructing hypotheses or ideas about how to solve the problem (3) testing these hypotheses and (4) analysing the results and drawing conclusions.

Social change - alteration of social structure in a given direction.

Social class - a social category with members in the same economic situation.

Socio-economic status - a social class as defined by one's level of education, income and occupation.

Social interaction - action that mutually affects two or more individuals.

Social mobility - the movement of individuals from lower to higher (upward mobility) or higher to lower (downward mobility) social categories in a social stratification.

Socialisation - the process by which the individual develops a personality structure and culture is transmitted from one generation to the next.

Society - a group who share the same culture occupying a territory.

Sociology - the science of society.

Sociology of education - a specialized field of knowledge emphasizing the relationship between education and society.

Status - degree of honour or prestige given by or received from society.

Stereotypes - conventional or over simplified beliefs.

Strata - social categories within a stratification system.

Structural-functionalism - a theoretical orientation emphasizing the functions or contributions made to society by existing social structures.

Symbol - any phenomenon such as an object, design or sound that represents something other than itself.

Symbolic interactionism - a theoretical orientation focusing on the individual's definition of the situation, roles and self-image.

Theory - a system of tentative ideas, concepts or statements about how to solve a problem or about the nature of reality.

Traditional education - a system of education emphasizing the transmission of knowledge, skills and moral training that conforms to past norms and values.

Value - a goal widely shared within society (or a subgroup of society).

Variable - a characteristic that may vary or change from one situation to another.

Appendix

Erickson's Eight Stages of Human Development

Stage of human Development	Age period	Characteristics to Be Achieved	Major Hazards to Achievement
Trust versus mistrust	Birth to 1 year	Sense of trust or security – achieved through parental gratification of needs and affection.	Neglect, abuse, or deprivation; inconsistent or inappropriate love in infancy; early or harsh weaning.
Autonomy versus shame and doubt	1 to 4 years	Sense of autonomy – achieved as child begins to see self as individual apart from his/her parents.	Conditions that make the child feel inadequate, evil, or dirty.
Initiative versus guilt	4 to 5 years	Sense of initiative-achieved as child begins to imitate adult behaviour and extends control of the world around him/her.	Guilt produced by overly strict discipline and the internalisation of rigid ethical standards that interfere with the child's spontaneity.
Industry versus inferiority	6 to 12 years	Sense of duty and accomplished- achieved as the child lays and begins to undertake tasks and schoolwork.	Feelings of inadequacy produced by excessive competition, personal limitations, or other events leading to feelings of inferiority.

Erickson's Eight Stages of Human Development (continued)

Identity versus role confusion	Adolescence	Sense of identity-achieved as one clarifies sense of self and what he/she believes in.	Sense of role confusion resulting from the failure of the family or society to provide clear role models.
Intimacy versus isolation	Young adulthood	Sense of intimacy-the ability to establish close personal relationships with others.	Problems with earlier stages that make it difficult to get close to others.
Generativist versus stagnation	30s to 50s	Sense of productivity and creativity resulting from work and parenting activities.	Sense of stagnation produced by feeling inadequate as a parent and stifled at work.
Integrity versus despair	Old age	Sense of ego integrity-achieved by acceptance of the life one has lived.	Feeling of despair and dissatisfaction with one's role as a senior member of society.

Source: Erickson, Erick. (1963). Childhood and Society. New York: Norton.

The stages of socialisation outlined by Erickson strongly suggest that socialisation is a life long process and that each stage has challenges. In addition, social and cultural practices influence the type of persons we become.

Index

Academic performance
  and social class, 113
Adolescence
  characteristics of, 58
Adult education, 146
African Indigenous
  Education, 191
  concept of, 69
African indigenous peoples, 81
African Indigenous Societies, 79
  in pre-colonial era, 77
  moral education, 77
Agencies of socialization, xi
Agikuyu, 101
AIDS, 95
Anomie, 191
Anthropology, 15
Authoritarianism, 40
Authority
  and discipline, 131
Bourgeoisies, 112
Capitalism, 40
Caste system, 108, 191
Census, 191
Charismatic authority, 191
Christ, Jesus, 11
Christendom, 171
Circumcision, 73. *See also* rites of passage
Classless society, 191
Classroom
  characteristics, 123
Comte, Auguste, 1, 3, 30
  and positive philosophy, 4
  contribution to sociology, 5
  stages of development, 4
Conflict theorists, 36, 37, 50
Conflict theory, 191
  assumptions, 36
  criticism of, 38
  definition, 35
  functions of, 37
  implications to education, 37
  proponents, 35
Consensus theorist, 50
Contest mobility, 191
Cultural transmission
  and education, 99
Culture, 91, 96, 191
  and education, 91
  and the school curriculum, 102
  characteristics of, 98
  definition, 78
Curriculum
  formal, 150
  hidden, 150
  meaning, 71
Darwin, Charles, 6
Dependent variable, 192
Dewey, John, 19, 23
Diffusion
  and cultural change, 95
Direct teachers, 127
Durkheim, Emile, 3, 7, 19, 30
  contribution to education, 21
  contributions of, 9
  types of societies, 9
Ebola, 95
Economics, 15

Education
  and social stratification
    in colonial Africa, 116
    in post colonial Era, 116
  formal, 70
  functions, 100
  informal, 70
  system, 153
Education and social
  stratification, 107
Educational opportunity, 112
Educational performance
  factors and their effects, 114
Educational sociology. *See*
  Sociology of education
Electra complex, 57
Empiricism, 14
Employment opportunities,
  153
  and Gender, 153
Enculturation, 70, 78, 98
Endogamous cultural change,
  93
Equality of Educational
  Opportunity, 192
Erickson, Erick, 197
  Eight Stages of Human
  Development, 196
Ethnomethodology, 192
  meaning of, 43
  theory, 43
Evolutionary theory, 192
Exchange and labelling
  theorists, 51
Exchange theory, 41, 192
Exogamous cultural change,
  95
Feminism
  history, 44
  meaning of, 44
Feminist movement, 45
Feminist sociologists, 45
Feminist theories
  and education, 44
Feudal societies, 112
Fidello, Custro, 94
Flanders, 127
  categorization of teachers, 128
Forum for African Women
  Educationist (FAWE), 143
Functional theory
  implications to education, 32
Functionalist theory
  criticism of, 34
Gandhi, Mahatma, 10
Gender, 192
  and education disparity, 143
  and the hidden curriculum,
    150
  concept of, 141
  education gap, 145
  roles, 61
  sex, 141
    concept of, 141
Genital mutilation
  also female circumcision, 73
Girls education, 147
Harambee philosophy, 94, 99
Herzberg, 176
Hidden curriculum, 193
HIV/AIDS, 87
Homans, George, 42
Hypothesis, 193
Independent variable, 193
Indigenous education, 69
  curriculum, 71

decline, 73
emphasis, 70
goals, 70
methods of instruction, 72
purpose, 70
versus western education, 74
Indirect teachers, 128
Industrial societies, 112
Interaction dynamics, 133
Jacobson, 40
Jensen, 26
Journal of Educational Sociology, 25
Journal of Sociology of Education, 25
Jua Kali sector, 100
Kambas, 101
Kenya Certificate of Secondary Education (KCSE), 173
Kenya Institute of Education (KIE), 187
Kenya National Examination Council (KNEC), 187
Kenya National Union of Teachers (KNUT), 162, 187
Kenya Science Teachers' College, 164
Kenya Technical Teachers College, 164
Kenyan social classes, 109
Kenyatta, Jomo, 11
Kibera, Lucy Wairimu, iii
Kimokoti, Agnes, iii
Kisii, 101
Labelling theory, 40, 135

Laissez-faire, 125
Leadership
definition, 124
styles, 124
Learner-centred method, 128
Lenin, 94
Lewin's research, 125
Liberal feminism, 45
Liberalism, 40
Luos, 101
Maasai, 101
Management
definition, 131
Mannheim, Karl, 19, 22
Mao, Tse Tung, 94
Marx, Karl, 11, 35
and Capital, 12
and Communist Manifesto, 11
and social class, 111
Marxist socialist feminism
perspective, 46
Mass media
and socialization, 63
Material culture, 92
Mead, George Herbert, 39
Mohamed, the prophet, 11
Moral education in modern Africa
teaching challenges, 84
Moral education in pre-colonial Africa, 83
Morality
definition, 77
Mores, 193
National schools, 114
National Society for the Study of Education Sociology, 25

None-physical initiation ceremony, 87
Non-mater culture, 92
Norm, 193
Nuclear family, 60
Oedipus
　complex, 57
　conflict, 57
　crisis, 57
Operational definitions, 193
Parsons, Talcott, 30
Peer groups, 193
　influences, 63
Political science, 16
Polyandry, 60
Polygamy, 60
Positive Philosophy, 4
Post-secondary educational institutions, 145
Pre-primary education
　enrolment, 144
Primary schools
　enrolment, 144
Primary socialization, 55
Probability sampling, 193
Proletariat, 112
Psychology, 15
Radical feminism, 47
　criticism of, 50
Report of the Civil Service Committee, 186
Report of the Civil Service Review Committee, 186
Report of the Commission of Inquiry, 186
Revolution, 193
Rites of passage, 82. *See also* circumcision
Rosenthal, 40
Sampling procedures, 194
School curriculum, 62
School education
　encouragement, 115
Scientific methods, 194
Secondary schools
　enrolment, 145
Severe Acute Respiratory Syndrome (SARS), 95
Sex role identification, 58
Sexism, 194
　ideology, 143
Sheng, 92, 136
Single parent family, 61
Social class, 194
　definitions of, 111
Social interaction, 194
Social mobility, 194
Social psychology, 15
Social stratification
　definition of, 107
　types of, 107
Socialisation, 194
　process, 55
Socialism, 12
　shortcomings, 12
Socialization
　agents of, 59
　meaning of, 55
Socialization and education, 65
Socializees, 59
Society
　definition of, 2
Socio-economic status, 194

Sociological theory
  definition of, 13
Sociology
  and other social sciences, 14
  as a discipline, 1
  definition of, 1
  development of, 3
  scope of, 13
Sociology of Education, 194
  concerns of, 26
  definition of, 19
Sociology of the classroom, 123
Sociometric test, 136
Sociometrists, 137
Sociometry technique, 136
Spencer, Herbert, 3, 6, 30
Structural - functionalism, 195
Structural-Functionalism/ Consensus, 29
Student teacher, 174
Symbolic interaction, 50
Symbolic interaction theory, 39
  weaknesses of, 43
Symbolic interactionism, 195
Systems of marriage, 148
Teacher
  and classroom management, 131
  and education, 174
  centred approaches, 128
  expectations, 129
  perception, 170
  roles, 166–69
  social roles, 169
  the changing multiple roles, 166
Teacher-pupil interactions, 123
Teachers
  and teaching career attitudes, 165
  categories in Kenya, 164
Teachers Service Commission (TSC), 162, 187
Teaching methods, 127
Teaching profession, 159
  improvement ways, 188
  joining, 173
  status, 185
Traditional education, 195
United Kingdom's social categories, 110
Value of Interaction theory to education, 42
Weber
  concept of bureaucratisation, 10
  types of leadership, 10
Weber Max, 1, 3, 10, 38
Youth culture, 92

www.ingramcontent.com/pod-product-compliance
Lightning Source LLC
Chambersburg PA
CBHW021404290426
44108CB00010B/383